Crime as Destiny

First published in 1931, *Crime as Destiny* throws a beam of light across the darkness which enshrouds the study of the deeper causes of crime and the eternal debate between nature versus nurture. The author's investigations led him to conclusions of the first importance to the sociologist and the psychologist. But the subject is wilder than it seems and by its direct bearing on the question of determinism will arouse the interest of the theologian and the student of philosophy as well. For the student of history, this research work will help trace the beginning of the logic of eugenics that will eventually take its nightmarish form under Hitler.

I0127788

Crime as Destiny

A Study of Criminal Twins

Johannes Lange

Routledge
Taylor & Francis Group

LONDON AND NEW YORK

First published in 1931
by George Allen & Unwin Ltd

This edition first published in 2022 by Routledge
4 Park Square, Milton Park, Abingdon, Oxon, OX14 4RN
and by Routledge
605 Third Avenue, New York, NY 10017

Routledge is an imprint of the Taylor & Francis Group, an informa business

Publisher's Note
The publisher has gone to great lengths to ensure the quality of this reprint but points
out that some imperfections in the original copies may be apparent.

Disclaimer
The publisher has made every effort to trace copyright holders and welcomes
correspondence from those they have been unable to contact.

A Library of Congress record exists under LCCN: 32019372

ISBN: 978-1-032-35078-3 (hbk)
ISBN: 978-1-003-32522-2 (ebk)
ISBN: 978-1-032-35087-5 (pbk)

Book DOI 10.4324/9781003325222

CRIME AS DESTINY

A STUDY OF CRIMINAL TWINS

by

PROF. DR. JOHANNES LANGE

*Physician-in-Chief at the Munich-Schwabing
Hospital, and Departmental Director of the
German Experimental Station for
Psychiatry (Kaiser Wilhelm In-
stitute) in Munich*

FOREWORD BY J. B. S. HALDANE

*Fullerian Professor of Physiology,
Royal Institution, London, etc.*

TRANSLATED BY

CHARLOTTE HALDANE

LONDON
GEORGE ALLEN & UNWIN LTD
MUSEUM STREET

The German original "Verbrechen als Schicksal, Studien an Kriminellen Zwillingen," was published by Georg Thieme Verlag in Leipzig in 1929

FIRST PUBLISHED IN GREAT BRITAIN IN 1931

PRINTED IN GREAT BRITAIN BY
UNWIN BROTHERS LTD., WOKING

TRANSLATOR'S NOTE

My first intention, and that of the publishers, was that I should make a fairly free translation of this book. When, however, I began my task, I decided to stick as closely as possible to the original text. There were two reasons for this change of plan. The more carefully I studied Professor Lange's work, the more I became convinced of the importance, not only of the whole, but of every sentence, almost every word, in it. It seemed to me that a free translation might easily degenerate into bowdlerisation, and that in view of its scientific importance such a method would do it less than justice. I was convinced also that in view of Professor Lange's most unusual gift for racy, descriptive narrative, such a course was unnecessary. I have tried to convey the charm of his conversational, sometimes purposely slangy and humorous style, which transforms some of the biographies of his subjects, notably the Heufelders and the Lauterbachs, into fragments of literature as impressive as certain pages of Dostoievsky or Thackeray. But Professor Lange's stories have the additional fascination of truth. The plain facts stated, together with the author's exceptional imaginative sympathy with his subjects, could not be improved upon by any translator.

CHARLOTTE HALDANE

FOREWORD

By J. B. S. HALDANE

FULLERIAN PROFESSOR OF PHYSIOLOGY,
ROYAL INSTITUTION, LONDON, ETC.

Why do people commit crimes? This question has been asked, and answered, ever since we have any records of human thought. In the Bible we find answers of various kinds. Evil acts are sometimes put down to supernatural intervention, as when the serpent tempted Eve and the Lord hardened Pharaoh's heart. Sometimes they are ascribed to the influence of other men, as when Jeroboam, the son of Nebat, made Israel to sin. In other passages the source of evil is placed quite as emphatically within us. According to Jeremiah, "The heart is deceitful above all things, and desperately wicked: who can know it?" And Jesus said, "Out of the heart proceed evil thoughts, murders, adulteries, fornications, thefts, false witness, blasphemies: these are the things which defile a man."

Now in the Bible spiritual things are described in parables—that is to say, symbolically. We know to-day that the heart has very little to do with moral behaviour. Heart disease does not lead to evil conduct. Brain disease, especially lethargic encephalitis, often does so. This fact is generally realised. In the same way we shall gradually come to see that spatial metaphors, like "inside" or "external", though at first useful, are ultimately misleading when applied to the mind. If we treat the mind like a box and say that some things are outside it and others within it, we are ultimately led into contradictions.

The scientific approach to the problem of evil is of a different character. The secret of success in scientific research lies largely in asking simple questions. We do not say, "What is matter?" but "What are the differences in behaviour between different sorts of matter?" and the answer even to that question is the whole science of chemistry. We do, incidentally, get from chemistry a partial answer to what matter is, but the chemist, in his individual researches, always asks much simpler questions than this.

Just the same is true in scientific psychology, of which Professor Lange's book is a masterpiece. He does not pose such terrific questions as that of the origin of evil or the nature of the will. He attempts to answer the question, "What accounts for certain resemblances and differences in human conduct?" And no one who reads this book through can deny that he has answered it with a fair measure of success.

When we compare two human beings or, for the matter of that, two animals or plants, we can put down all the differences between them to one of four sets of causes:

1. Differences of ancestry,
2. Segregation,
3. Differences of environment,
4. Uncaused events, if such occur.

Let me explain what I mean. Two brothers, or two seedlings from the same plant, generally resemble one another more closely than two individuals taken at random from the population. This is because they have the same ancestry. But even two brothers may differ a great deal. This is due to a phenomenon called segregation. If you want to see segregation at work, look at an average litter of kittens. Segregation takes place as follows. Every man or woman has in each nucleus of every cell in his or her body two sets of genes, ultra-microscopic bodies which determine the innate differences between people. When germ cells (eggs and spermatozoa) are formed, only a single set of genes goes into each cell, and these genes are chosen more or less at random from the two parental sets. The union of two germ cells gives a new individual with a double set of genes.

How can we avoid segregation and get a set of individuals each of whom carries the same genes? This is how the fruit-breeder does it. He self-fertilises one apple-tree or crosses two, thus getting a number of seeds. Of a thousand seedling trees only one may be worth preserving. This one is multiplied by cutting and grafting, and the trees derived in this way are all extraordinarily alike because they are really sections of a single tree. The world contains several million trees of Cox's Orange Pippin, but from the point of view of the geneticist they are a single individual. Thus, if we can find a case of reproduction apart from the sexual process, we shall be able to avoid segregation.

But we cannot propagate men and women from cuttings. Solomon's suggested experiment in this direction was abandoned owing to opposition from the mother of the subject. However, nature often succeeds where Solomon failed. The human egg cell divides into two soon after fertilisation. Usually the two halves stay together, each growing into one-half of the embryo; occasionally they are separated, and form two twin embryos. These resemble one another as do two cuttings from the same apple- or rose-tree. Ordinary twins are no more alike than brothers or sisters born separately. But monozygotic twins, as the products of fission of an egg are called, are physically so like that their own mother often cannot tell them apart. For example, the right hands of such a pair are more alike, as judged by finger-prints, than the right and left hand of the same person. The first two sets of causes are abolished in them. Moreover, their environments in childhood at least are extraordinarily similar. Differences in their behaviour must be due to minor environmental differences and to events of the fourth class in our list.

That fourth class includes free-will if it is taken in the sense of indeterminism, or action independent of any causes. It may be a class with no members, like the snakes of Ireland; but it would, I think, be unscientific to leave it out of consideration altogether. Theologians are, of course, sharply divided as to whether free-will exists or not. All Catholics and some Protestants and Mohammedans believe in it. Calvinists and most Mohammedans reject it as being a limitation on the omnipotence of God. If we regard the laws of nature as the manifestation of God's will, this point of view is essentially that of most scientists to-day.

Professor Lange's answer to the question is, I think, decisive. The human characteristics with which he is concerned are those moral decisions which land us in or out of prison. Given two twins derived from the same fertilised egg and brought up together, at least in early childhood, what degree of similarity is shown in their moral decisions? He investigated thirteen pairs in which one brother or sister was a criminal. In ten out of the thirteen the other was a criminal too. Professor Lange, like a true scientist, has weighted the evidence against himself. I think that, on the evidence provided in his book, he might quite well have excluded his last pair, the Landsknecht brothers, of whom only one was a criminal, from his monozygotic twins, and classed them with the Garkoch brothers as doubtful cases. The Maat brothers, of whom one had been convicted and the other was a fugitive from justice, might also have been omitted on the ground of incomplete information. This would leave us with nine concordant and two discordant pairs, a rather more striking degree of resemblance than that actually found. When we examine the two undeniable cases of monozygotic pairs where one only was a criminal, we find that in each case the criminal brother had suffered from a severe head injury. In the case of the other discordant pair, the Landsknechts, one, but not the other, suffered from goitre, a disease which undoubtedly alters the character.

To sum up—an analysis of the thirteen cases shows not the faintest evidence of freedom of the will in the ordinary sense of that word. A man of a certain constitution, put in a certain environment, will be a criminal. Taking the record of any criminal, we could predict the behaviour of a monozygotic twin placed in the same environment. *Crime is destiny*. The defenders of indeterminism could at most claim that free-will very occasionally tipped the balance over, and thus counted for something in the long run, but not often enough for its effects to appear in a series of a dozen cases taken at random. And a free-will of this kind is clearly of no practical importance.

But is this resemblance largely caused by environment? What sort of similarity is found in the conduct of twins who, though born and bred together and therefore sharing a similar environment since their conception, have arisen from two separate eggs, and carry different sets of genes? Professor Lange examined seventeen such pairs, of which one was a criminal. In only two cases was the other a criminal as well, and one of these pairs, the Garkochs, may really have been monozygotic. They have been included here because Professor Lange quite rightly weights the evidence against his own theory. Putting the figures thus:

	Concordant.	Discordant.
Monozygotic	10	3
Dizygotic	2	15

the odds that they are significant of a real difference are about seven thousand to one. This is an under-estimate, because all the known facts about twins point in the same direction. Clearly to obtain identical behaviour one must have not only the same ancestry and the same environment, but the same set of genes dealt out by segregation.

To get a complete story we should want yet a third class of records, namely, of monozygotic twins who had been separated from early infancy. These are much harder to obtain. So far as I know only four such cases have been investigated, namely, by Professors Muller, of Austin, Texas, and Newman, of Chicago, whose results are published in the *Journal of Heredity*. Unfortunately, none of the eight people concerned were criminals. But as a result of their different upbringings they did show markedly greater divergences, both of character and intellect, than extreme believers in the omnipotence of "heredity" would care to admit. In spite of this the resemblances were striking. As Professor Lange states, about half his criminals, in the concordant dizygotic pairs, would probably have grown up into decent or at least harmless citizens if placed in suitable environments. It is difficult to imagine that the Lauterbachs or Heufelders could easily have been turned into pillars of society. But the case of Luitpold Schweizer shows that the influence of a woman can redeem one of a pair of criminals, and could, in all probability, have kept him from crime.

On the whole, Professor Lange preserves an extra-

ordinarily objective attitude to his subject, but even he
is human, as appears from the emotions aroused in him
by the Maat brothers and by motor-cyclists. And it must
be emphasised that the special views as to the nature of
the breakdown which occurs in criminals, as stated in the
Conclusion, are not supported by the same weight of
evidence as his main thesis. Again, his views on the
importance of alcoholism as a factor in crime are probably
true for Bavaria, where beer is consumed in quantities
whose mere mention would ruin any reputation which I
may have for accuracy. But it is equally clear that in
England, which has dealt pretty successfully with the
problem of alcohol, its consumption is not a major cause
of criminal behaviour. In the United States the connection may well be closer.

What would be the effect on human conduct if the view
that crime is destiny were generally adopted? Supporters
of indeterminism state that a belief in fatalism should
logically yield to a blind acceptance of events and a
refusal to struggle either against external circumstances
or defects of character. I cannot myself see the cogency
of this view. My will may not be free in certain senses
of that word, but it is at least my own. I regard my
character and my environment as equally predestined,
and get quite a lot of quiet fun out of the attempt to
prove that the former is the more important. As a matter
of historical fact, fatalism does not conduce to weakness of
will. The opposite is true. Among the ranks of the fatalists
must be reckoned Mohammed and his successors, who

conquered from the Atlantic to the Indus in a century, the leaders of the Reformation, the founders of the New England States, Napoleon, Lenin, and Trotsky. Clearly a belief in destiny is rather a help than a hindrance to a character already strong.

But, it is often urged, the man of weak will becomes still weaker if he believes that his failures are predestined. I do not think that this is the fact. Quite as often a man who recognises his weaknesses arranges his life so as to avoid situations which he knows he cannot face. Mr. Smith does not frequent places where he is offered drink, because he knows he cannot resist it. For a similar reason Mr. Jones avoids ladies who say that their husbands misunderstand them. We all have our weak spots, and it is well worth sowing a few wild oats if we can find out what they are and act upon the knowledge. The consistent believer in free-will repents, and hopes that his will may keep him out of the same sin in the future. The intelligent fatalist regards his lapses with a certain tolerance, but acts on the knowledge of his own character which he gains through them.

This point of view is well borne out by a comparison of Catholic and non-Catholic Europeans. The former believe in free-will and the duty of periodic repentance. They believe that the one real evil is sin—that is to say, a bad will. The latter, whether Protestants or Freethinkers, mostly believe that there are other evils besides sin, for example, poverty, disease, and war. They are often determinists, and are not in the habit of confessing

B

their sins. They believe that evil can be fought, not only
by working on the individual will, but by social legislation.
For them good conduct is worth while, even if it is
brought about by legislation and not by a change of
heart. And their beliefs have, as a matter of fact, been
pretty successful in practice. The criminal statistics of
England and Wales are rather striking in this respect.
It is not known what proportion of the population are
Catholics. The members of that organisation claim
8 per cent., but only $5\frac{1}{2}$ per cent. of marriages are cele-
brated with Catholic rites, although Catholics who marry
out of their religion are commanded to do so in a Catholic
church, and generally comply. But 15 per cent. of our
criminals are Catholics. So a Catholic is at least twice as
likely to become a criminal as a member of another
religion or of none. This is not a very good advertisement
for the value of the belief in free-will as a practical guide
to conduct. Catholic apologists like Mr. Chesterton dis-
miss facts like those brought forward by Professor Lange
as "Cruel stories of curse in bone and kin". Unfortunately
the stories happen to be true. You cannot overcome evils
by saying that they do not exist.

So much for the individual. But what would be our
attitude to the errors of our fellows if we adopted a strict
determinism as a general view of life? To answer that
question we must first remember an elementary fact.
Praise and blame, which are very powerful social motives,
are largely reserved for those sides of conduct which
they can in fact influence. We blame people for being

lazy or vicious, and this does on the whole have an effect in making them more industrious and sober. We do not blame them for being stupid or physically weak, and it would be useless to do so. But the fact that certain sides of conduct can be influenced in this way need not lead us into dubious metaphysics. The determinist will go on blaming his erring brother, but the blame will be more than half pity. And he will avoid moral indignation. I find certain kinds of conduct in others disgusting, but there is no reason why I should lose my temper about them. And I know that an attitude of moral indignation is peculiarly ineffective in bringing about a change of heart in others. On the contrary, it is an ideal excuse for cruelty. The newspapers are full of letters from virtuous persons who demand corporal punishment for such offences as cruelty to animals or children. Their writers do not seem to realise that they are putting themselves on the moral level of those they condemn.

We have got to reshape our attitude to evil. An acceptance of the results of such work as that of Professor Lange will lead us to realise that every evil has a cause. If we desire that the fight against evil should be more successful in the future than it has been in the past, our first duty is to find out these causes; and a perusal of *Crime as Destiny* will make it clear that for that task we need every resource of science. Until we know very much more than anyone knows to-day we shall be working in the dark. But no one in our generation has done more to dispel that darkness than Professor Lange.

PREFACE

In giving this little book the title *Crime as Destiny*, I am aware that I shall challenge much opposition. I am not thinking of the fact that the heading may appear to some unsuitable to a sober investigation; that I take for granted. I expect it rather from those whose views on life are diametrically opposed to the conception of crime indicated by this title. Nevertheless the biologist, and still more the doctor who has to deal with the individual criminal, cannot help again and again seeing fate in crime, stronger than the individual with his "free-will". The natural tendencies one is born with, the surrounding world he grows up in—these are essentials, are destiny; and it is also destiny which decides how the environment with its numberless influences is going to shape the natural tendencies into one whole.

In dealing with the individual criminal, the doctor will always consider his natural tendencies first—that unalterable material which so often breaks down all efforts to help and which forces one to consider criminal conduct as a symptom of abnormal make-up.

But this view of the criminal is not by any means common to all medical men; it is not the "natural one"—we all carry far too many memories about with us—and it is finally not the whole of the medical conception of the problem of crime. The doctor has not alone to serve the individual, he has always to think of the general problem, of the public interest. If we are unable to help the individual criminal we must ask ourselves whether it is not possible to safeguard the public and thus to avoid the misery of the individual. Therefore we at once add a question-mark to the title *Crime as Destiny*. In this sense opposition is wanted and deliberately sought. May we not hope that it will be possible in future to prevent the birth of a large number of people whose natural tendencies turn them into criminals under our present system?

At the same time it is suggested that crime cannot be simply destiny in another sense. Our present conditions, and especially the steps we take for the prevention of crime, are not unalterable, and I think that changes in this field could prevent more than one crime. In a double sense, therefore, fate is in our hands.

But I cannot go farther into this question, nor will my investigations have solved any problem. But I shall bring forward facts which I hope will give plenty of material for reflection. As what I have to communicate concerns not only medical practitioners but the general public as well, I have kept only to the most essential medical terms and have expressed myself in the simplest possible manner. The real importance of this little book lies in the problem it raises and the individual destinies it describes, and not in what I myself have added thereto. I hope it will arouse a deeper insight and at the same time prepare the way to help.

I have to express my special thanks to Herr Ministe- rialrat Dr. Degen, of the Bavarian Ministry of Justice,

and Herr Obermedizinalrat Dr. Viernstein, Director of
the Institute for Criminal Biology at Straubing Prison,
who have assisted this investigation in every possible way.
Without the Institute for Criminal Biology and the
organisation connected with it, this research would hardly
have been possible as matters stand to-day.

JOHANNES LANGE

MUNICH,
  September 15, 1928

CONTENTS

————————————

ILLUSTRATIONS

CRIME AS DESTINY

I

INTRODUCTION

"It would be an . . . improvement of our present-day
justice if every year a lottery were held among all citizens
of this free land of ours in order to decide who should
go to prison and who should not. The result of the draw
would represent just as impartial a form of justice as the
one we now have, and would also give each of us an
opportunity for once to be punished and reformed as a
miserable sinner. God would keep an eye on the matter
and would take care that even those who had not drawn
prison as their lot would receive what they deserved."
Thus writes Lindsey, a judge of the American children's
courts, and according to his alleged, though not altogether
likely, experiences he ought to know. God, before whom
we are all guilty, is his witness, and for those whose life
is poised between mercy and hell, Lindsey's words
certainly must have a deep meaning. Lindsey also says
nothing which they will straightway deny to the many
who have unmitigated insight into the phenomena on the
edge of their consciousness and into the final bases of
their conduct, and who have nevertheless not been able
to free themselves.

In Germany as well as in America many earnest people
incline to views which come very close to those of the
American judge of youth. According to such views the
criminal is set apart from the mass of humanity, not by

the stock he springs from, but by accidental and difficult circumstances which control his life-history. The blame is chiefly put on experiences in early childhood and unpropitious influences as regards education. In this way society is most to blame for crime and the criminal. He is at bottom a martyr who only needs our keenest sympathy, as well as help, education, and training, to become as good a member of human society as anyone else.

"All things are good as they came out of the hands of their Creator, but everything degenerates in the hands of man." This famous statement of Rousseau's is accepted by more people to-day than was ever the case since it was written.

In other times people thought otherwise, and even to-day only very few would agree unconditionally with Lindsey. The view that human beings are intrinsically quite different from one another and that the environment given them by fate has only very small importance for the development of personality is another held quite bluntly and also by quite serious people. Galton once used the example of the cuckoo, who sings the same song in all parts of the world, although his eggs are laid in all kinds of different nests. The "continuous merciless march of the hidden weaknesses in our nature through sickness to death" and also in the spiritual sphere was what Galton's investigations revealed, and he considers it a fair question to ask whether environmental influences have any part at all in the development of personality apart from the fact that they facilitate knowledge and professional training. "One cannot avoid the conclusion that heredity has an enormously greater weight than environmental influences when the differences in the latter do not go beyond those commonly found between persons of the same class and the same country." Galton does not actually refer to the problem of the criminal, but it is indubitable that if his conclusions were correct they would have great importance in the field of criminology.

Such coarsely differentiated points of view are only possible where emotional reactions definitely influence the judgment. That emotional needs must play an important part in the question of how crimes come to be committed is obvious. Moral, religious, ethical, political considerations colour the question before one has even considered the facts. Taken alone, these could give one completely clear and undeniable conclusions without abolishing the contradictions of the various points of view. Galileo denied his incontestable discovery before the religious tribunal, and yet it was as certain as it had been before that the earth was the centre of the universe. But here, in the case of the problem of the criminal, even the facts are not completely clear. We do know numberless details but nothing conclusive.

Thus we know the quantitative relationship between certain social phenomena and crime; for example, the number of crimes against property rises during bad economic periods. Crimes of violence and sexual crimes have a definite yearly and even perhaps weekly curve, due to external causes, some of which we know. Therefore outward influences are certainly not without importance as causes of crime. On the other hand, we know criminal families who have been followed up for several generations and in whom the inclusion of bad as well as good blood

is revealed in an unmistakable manner. It has long ago
been shown that hardened criminals are not seldom
descended from criminal parents or else have numerous
criminal relations. We also know that hereditary taints,
such as mental diseases, and particularly alcoholism and
psychopathic disturbances, are very common in criminals,
and that many of them are themselves mentally sick or
otherwise abnormal. We know types of so little intelligence and so lacking in all social feeling that sooner or
later they simply must come up against the law. Owing
to the importance of this fact the chief interest in the
investigation of crime has shifted during recent years
more and more from the deed to the doer. In spite of
this the controversy as to whether unfavourable tendencies
or environment are mostly responsible for crime has not
been settled. At any rate, Lombroso's dream of "the
born criminal", "the natural delinquent", as a special
human type has been dreamed to a finish. Nothing
remains of it except the sterile fact that a large number
of criminals are in some way or another abnormal, just
as are many other people who never come into conflict
with the law at all.

We have hardly got a definite step beyond such general
observations. However much we may talk, we still do not
know enough about the great majority of criminals to
make certain of dealing with them successfully.

This situation is not very satisfactory from the point of
view of our civilisation. Decisions of the most far-reaching
importance are made quite blindly. We erect new legal
codes without having tackled the basic questions at all
seriously. We are getting rid of the concept of punishment. We take the most comprehensive precautions to

safeguard society, we sterilise thousands of criminals, and on the other hand we claim for a number of others protection on the ground of low powers of self-control which make them a danger to society, while we cannot know at all clearly who should be sterilised or who should be permanently protected. We have no means for the simplest collection and investigation of the real basic material which should precede any such measures.

That is the general position to-day, and yet in certain cases, at any rate, the possibility of taking a right or a false attitude to the problem rests with ourselves. Are we going to take a blind risk that in the future justice shall become less and less secure, that criminal tendencies (if there really are such things) shall be propagated without check, or shall we, on the other hand, destroy an irreplaceable hereditary material? Must we decide the question whether or not to abolish the death penalty entirely from the point of view of political expediency? I should have thought that any society would go to the limit of trouble to get this matter cleared up.

Actually the beginnings of reform can be seen in one or two places. Above all, a few educationists have set themselves to deal with young law-breakers partly through professional interest, partly through sympathy blended with such high ideals and so much self-sacrifice that when they have done all they can they will still put down failure to their own inadequacy rather than that of their charges. "We should be still more careful to educate from the child's point of view and to discover the roots of his tendencies in order to form his character according to his innate possibilities. We are still fumbling about far too much", was the answer given me by an admirable and admired woman when I ventured to criticise some of her work on the ground that she had made too much of inborn tendencies. If such humanists had their way every difficult adolescent would have more than one permanent guide to look after him, even though it were not at all certain that all the trouble taken would result in success. We can certainly not decide to-day whether it will be possible for any given individual to adapt himself successfully to social conditions.

As a preliminary to all intelligent measures we need wide and deep knowledge of criminals. In this field the State, with its huge organisations and materials, can do decisive work. And this task has been begun in a few places. Above all I must mention the Bavarian Ministry of Justice, which in spite of opposition has installed at Degen's instigation the Institute for Criminal Biology at Straubing Prison. Here are collected as many records as possible of criminals which have been thoroughly gone into by prison doctors in order to lay the basis of true knowledge. The number of investigators is a small one and the investigations have to be made in addition to routine work, which takes up almost all of the doctor's time. There is a dearth of people and means to make full use of the material collected, and with a curious failure to realise the importance of these investigations the State fails to provide money to improve the situation. Yet so much has been done that there is no place for destructive criticism. Those who criticise most loudly can bring up fewest facts to support them. Their own proposals can only be tested by the use of a mass of material which can be procured solely by the methods they attack. But it is a good sign that in spite of all criticism, many States are following the Bavarian example, and in other directions similar experiments are being made.

When we have really got a mass of material thoroughly investigated from all points of view, then we shall be able to deal with criminals with our eyes open. Until then we must go warily. However, there is one way—the way we have taken here—to clear up some basic questions more definitely than was hitherto possible. This is by the use of the so-called Twin method.

II

THE TWIN METHOD

Twins are brothers and sisters born together and who in the majority of cases have grown up together. In the decisive years of development they have had common experiences and have been subject to common educational influences. Apart from pairs consisting of a twin brother and a twin sister, there are pairs of twins of the same sex, but of quite different conception and formation.

The most famous example of one sort of twins of the same sex are Jacob and Esau, the sons of Isaac and Rebecca. They were not only different in appearance—Esau was red-skinned and rough, Jacob was fair and smooth—they had different voices and a different odour. In their tastes and their characters they differed equally. Esau was a hunter, rough, straightforward, uncontrolled, violent-tempered, and simple, and married wives of a lower class, sometimes against his father's orders; Jacob was a shepherd, smooth-speaking, artful, lying, out for his inheritance, and sly—at the same time tough, moody, and unjust. In choosing his brides he was cautious and self-sacrificing. The brothers were about as different from one another as sibs [1] could possibly be. Twins as different as these in appearance and character are quite common; they are called dizygotic twins, and there is good reason to suppose that they have been born from two ova which were simultaneously fertilised. According

[1] Sib is a collective name for all children born of the same parents.

to their innate dispositions they resemble or differ from one another about as much as ordinary sibs.

On the other hand, there are twins of the same sex who look so alike that it is almost impossible to tell them apart and whose personalities are also practically identical. According to general opinion, they have both sprung from one and the same fertilised egg and have therefore exactly the same hereditary disposition. A well-known example in literature are the brothers Weidelich in Gottfried Keller's *Martin Salander*. I suspect that they were drawn from life. They were as like as one egg is to another; in their behaviour they were also exactly similar. Independently both committed deceptions at the same time and in the same way. Outwardly they were just a little different according to circumstances.

The first person to think of using monozygotic and dizygotic twins to solve the problem of heredity and environment was Galton, who in 1876 published results which are still important to-day. He chose two different lines of investigation, taking first very similar, i.e. monozygotic, twins in order to see what possible differences later developed between them, and then very dissimilar, i.e. dizygotic, twins in order to find out whether the same outward influences increased their resemblance. He came to the conclusion already mentioned, that heredity has a far greater influence than environment. Twins with the same heredity seldom become different from one another, and if they do the difference is not due to "free-will". This was never denied by Galton's numerous clerical informants. On the other hand, similar experiences did not increase the resemblance between dizygotic twins.

Increasing experience has shown more and more clearly

that twins with markedly similar outward appearance
agree with one another in a large number of definite
characteristics, such as the colour and type of their hair,
eye colour, skin colour, distribution of body hair, etc.,
whereas with dizygotic twins these characteristics are
like those of other sibs, i.e. they are very seldom
exactly similar, or, if some may be, the whole lot never
are. Further, it was found out that monozygotic twins
always had the same hereditary diseases or else both
would remain free from family troubles, whereas non-
identical twins were in this respect like their other
brothers and sisters, i.e. they might both be ill at the
same time, but this did not happen more often than one
would expect, and mostly only one of the twins fell ill
while the other remained well. For it is inborn tendencies
which control the appearance of hereditary diseases, and
inborn tendencies are exactly the same in monozygotic
twins, but different in the dizygotic pairs. In the case of
the latter, in view of their similar parentage about half
the innate tendencies are the same.

Now there are diseases which are not exclusively due
to heredity but in whose case outward circumstances
play an important rôle. With regard to these, monozygotic
and dizygotic twins show characteristic differences. The
greater the weight of heredity, the more closely each of
a given pair of monozygotic twins will resemble one
another; as the importance of heredity is reduced the
susceptibility of monozygotic twins will resemble that
of two or more children born at the same time from
separately fertilised eggs.

The resemblances between monozygotic twins do not
stop at physical characteristics or disease; there are

remarkable resemblances on the mental plane. It is very rare to find human beings who are really identical from this point of view—for example, their writing is generally different—but it has been found that exactly similar attitudes on the part of monozygotic twins towards essential matters, such as a career or marriage, or their general relationship to their environment, are extremely common. Here again similar heredity plays its part. Hereditary nervous and mental troubles affect both of a pair of monozygotic twins almost without exception, or else both escape them.

All this justifies us in using the results obtained with twins in order to examine the question whether, and if so to what extent, experiences of the most different kinds are determined by our inborn tendencies. Siemens especially has systematically and successfully used this method. Complete agreement in the case of closely resembling twins backs up the view that heredity is chiefly, or at any rate preponderantly, responsible for one's experience. According to how much the behaviour of hereditarily identical twins differs, by just so much is the influence of heredity in determining our fate diminished.

III

USE OF THE TWIN METHOD IN INVESTIGATING
THE CAUSES OF CRIME

A. General

It was fairly obvious that the Twin method could be used to determine the influence of innate tendencies in the causation of crime. If the hereditary make-up had no importance, a comparison between monozygotic and dizygotic pairs of twins ought to show no differences. Agreement between the behaviour of monozygotic twins would be in accordance with the importance of heredity. A lack of agreement in the case of twins with identical heredity would enable us to estimate the importance of environmental incentives to crime. Finally, we could compare the behaviour of dizygotic twins with that of other brothers and sisters. If in comparison with other brothers and sisters twins with a different heredity showed closer agreement as far as crime was concerned, the importance of the environmental influences would be shown to be increased in proportion, as the latter can only be considered exactly similar in the case of those who have grown up together.

B. Material

Twins are not very common; roughly speaking, one pair is born to every eighty ordinary births. In addition, about 40 per cent. of twins die, a far higher percentage mortality than that of average children, owing to their weakness in infancy. The only twins considered suitable for our investigation were those who were both old enough to be prosecuted by the law; for it very often happens that one or the other twin dies young. Brother and sister pairs did not count for us, as it is well known that the differences between the sexes, as far as crime is concerned, are very great. Thus we had to find one of a pair who had been imprisoned and whose other twin was still living, was old enough to be able to come in conflict with the law, and was of the same sex.

The material was provided by the records of the Institute for Criminal Biology. Furthermore, at our request the Bavarian Ministry of Justice ordered that all prisoners in Bavarian prisons who were twins should be reported and examined from the point of view of Criminal Biology. In addition we also asked for such prisoners as had twins among their brothers and sisters who might also be of an age to be sentenced. Finally, I looked among the psychopathic patients of the Genealogical Department of the German Institute for Psychiatry for twins who had been imprisoned. I also asked all twins whom I met in the course of my hospital duties for criminal records. All those twins who fulfilled the above-mentioned conditions were taken as subjects. First of all, the criminal records of the subjects themselves and of their twin were examined. Then I interviewed those twins who were still in prisons. We then went into the degree of resemblance and the life-stories of all the subjects. Police records and sentences were, of course, examined at the same time. These were put at my disposal as well as other ordinary official documents. On various other pretexts I got some of the criminal twins to come for interviews to my consulting-room. Others I visited at their homes in different cities. My former colleague, Dr. Grüber, undertook particularly detailed researches at my request. I am also very grateful to Professor Ewald and Dr. Faltlhauser in Erlangen, Frau Dr. Schmidt-Kraepelin in Ludwigshafen, Fräulein Dr. Emy Metzgel in Frankfort, Fräulein Anny Weber in Burgebrach, and my colleagues Dr. Guttmann and Dr. Mosbacher for their valuable help.

All investigations had to be made with the greatest care, as in no case could we divulge the source of the addresses or the reasons for the questions asked. In order to avoid prejudices I did not even inform my helpers of what I was really after. Whenever I suspected myself of being prejudiced, I endeavoured to bring in other helpers, whom I entrusted with clearing up the question of personal resemblance, without, however, informing them of the criminal records. In this way I think I did all I could to keep the investigation free from subjective influences.

In a large number of cases I have exact measurements; in almost all of them several photographs, in a lot of them duplicate observations as well as finger-prints. In three cases it happened that twins who had been summoned to my consulting-room for other alleged reasons told me spontaneously in the course of a lengthy conversation about their conflicts with the law. In other cases this did not happen, and even in asking general questions I met with strong resistance. One or two pairs resisted all attempts at investigation, and gave either the most general or else unsatisfactory information. In other cases the question of monozygotism or dizygotism could not be cleared up satisfactorily owing to various difficulties. These cases I shall discuss later.

C. RESULTS

Thirty-seven pairs of twins were discovered and investigated in this way. In addition there were two other pairs, about whom I have a great deal of information, but whose derivation could not be ascertained.

The thirty-seven pairs included fifteen monozygotic and twenty-two dizygotic couples.

In two cases of monozygotics and five of dizygotics neither twin had been imprisoned—these were pairs discovered among the brothers and sisters of ordinary prisoners. These have nothing to do with our question. Otherwise I should have to include as material the many pairs among my other investigations into twins who have never been imprisoned.

This leaves us with thirty pairs—thirteen monozygotic and seventeen dizygotic, one of whom, i.e. the subject first investigated, had been imprisoned.

Among the thirteen monozygotic pairs the second twin was also imprisoned in ten cases, but in three cases had remained clear of the law. Among the seventeen dizygotic pairs the second twin had also been imprisoned in two cases. In fifteen cases this had not occurred. *This leads us to the following conclusion: as far as crime is concerned, monozygotic twins on the whole react in a definitely similar manner, dizygotic twins behave quite differently.* If, therefore, we attach importance to the twin method of investigation we must admit that as far as the *causes of crime are concerned, innate tendencies play a preponderant part.*

One pair of dizygotic twins, both of whom were

imprisoned, I should really place with the monozygotic. Two separate and reliable investigators took measurements which, together with photographs, showed complete agreement in unusual bodily characteristics, complexion, and so on. I am not including them because it is recorded that the twins were never taken for one another. This can be due to differences caused by environmental influences, to a different shape of the skull or the jaw-line, but I cannot be sure of it. I therefore prefer to leave them out.

I must just mention two pairs not included in the investigation. In one case they were twins of twenty-three years of age, one of whom stabbed the other to death. According to Par. 51 of the legal code the survivor was acquitted. No photographs of the victim exist. The relations are not intelligent, but they declare that there was a close resemblance between the two brothers. The record of the twin who was killed is apparently clean. But he was always threatening his twin, his other brothers and sisters, even his mother, with the knife, and like the survivor he was a bad lot.

Both brothers were feeble-minded, the survivor a little more than the dead one; both were hard of hearing and short-sighted. The living one was rather better-tempered and also more sentimental. Both of them had had many illnesses and had been badly knocked about by their drunken father. I saw the survivor and found there were still scars on his head. They were almost certainly monozygotic and should be classified with those whose conduct agreed.

The other pair were girls, now about twenty-four years old. Here are their records:

ANNA.   1. 1920. Lower Court. Unlicensed prostitution.
                    Two weeks' detention.
         2. 1922. Court of Jurors. Theft. Fourteen days'
                    imprisonment.
         3. 1924. Swindling. Four weeks' imprison-
                    ment.
         4. 1924. Giving false information as to identity.
                    Fourteen days' detention.

MARIA.   1. 1921 Court of Jurors. Theft. Five days'
                    imprisonment.
         2. 1922. Court of Jurors. Theft. Three weeks'
                    imprisonment.

In this case the results of investigation were meagre.
The twins themselves could not be got at. Their parents
did not reply to the letters sent them. The records of the
hospital where A. was taken were lost. The reformatories
to which both were sent could give us no information
with regard to our problem. We received helpful and
detailed information from their birthplace, but the twins
were there for a short time only. We do know that both
were of low intelligence and were very often ill, and that
they were apparently not extremely alike. One of them
had epileptic attacks. We have a clinical record of one of
them, but not much can be got out of it. Finally, we know
that the mother was a warehouse thief and systematically
taught the children to steal. This fact makes them
straightaway unsuitable as material, in any case so long
as they were still young. If classified at all on these facts
they would have to be added to the monozygotics of
similar behaviour.

I just want to mention the brother and sister pairs
about whom we accidentally got some information. In
nine cases the twin brother was sentenced but not the
twin sister. In one case the twin sister was imprisoned

several times for theft and swindling and was finally given four years for fraud. The twin brother, who was business manager of a large hotel, once incurred a small fine during the inflation period for putting up his prices contrary to the law; he had raised the price of beer one day earlier than the law allowed. In other ways his conduct was without fault, and he felt that he had been unjustly condemned, as he claimed to have made a mistake. In the last case, one of triplets, the sister of sixteen years was very heavily punished with eight days' detention for staying away from school, while the two brothers had clean records.

If, therefore, we analysed these cases as unfavourably as possible from the point of view of innate tendencies, the result would be as follows:

Among thirteen monozygotic pairs, ten would agree and three would disagree. Of thirty dizygotic pairs, five would agree and twenty-five would disagree.

If we distributed them according to what seems most highly probable, we should get the following proportions:

Of fifteen monozygotic pairs, twelve would agree and three would disagree; of twenty-eight dizygotic pairs, two would agree and twenty-six would disagree.

But these additions would not alter the basic proportions.

If we only took the numbers of which we are certain, the result would be that whereas 77 per cent. of monozygotic twins agree in their behaviour in relation to crime, only about 12 per cent. of the dizygotic twins do so. The proportions of these figures give some insight into the environmental influences, as does the lack of complete agreement of the figures regarding the monozygotics.

But such numerical calculations have no real value in such complicated cases.

D. COMPARISON BETWEEN DIZYGOTIC TWINS AND OTHER SIBS OF CRIMINALS

It is much more important to compare the criminality of ordinary brothers and sisters with that of dizygotic twins. If we found that among dizygotic twins both were punished more often than happened on an average among ordinary brothers and sisters, we should have to allow for the influence of environmental conditions more or less according to the degree of difference between expectations and the facts discovered. We had a number of facts on which to base such a comparison, for which we have to thank the Institute of Criminal Biology and its Director, Herr Obermedizinalrat Viernstein. In this case we were dealing exclusively with prisoners at Straubing, a homogeneous material consisting exclusively of males. To begin with, all the prisoners of a given year, i.e. 428, were questioned with regard to criminal sibs. These were found in 58 cases, and gave us 83 secondary cases, from which we subtracted the females as we were only examining relations of the same sex. There were 12 females in all, which left us with 71 cases of criminal sibs.

We then investigated the fertility of the families of a series of 200 prisoners born in wedlock. Including the criminals themselves, this gave us 1,546 children, from which we subtracted those who had died in infancy. According to Warstadt's results one must subtract one-quarter for these, which left approximately 1,160 living children. Further, the criminal subjects themselves had to be subtracted, whereby the number for comparison was further reduced to 960. As we were only dealing with brothers, the latter figure had to be halved. But even the remaining figure, namely, 480, was too high, as a lot of prisoners were still quite young and quite a large number would have younger brothers not yet of an age to be sentenced. So as we reckoned one-sixth for these, the final figures for comparison were 400 brothers for 200 convict subjects. In 428 families we found 71 secondary cases. Therefore, for 200 families we should obtain 33 secondary cases. According to this, among 400 brothers of criminals old enough to be prosecuted, we should expect 33 further criminals, i.e. one law-breaker in 12 brothers. Among the dizygotic twins we had, on the other hand, 2 criminals (i.e. about 1 in 8·5) for 17 pairs of twins.

The difference in the ratios 1 : 12 and 1 : 8·5 does not weigh very heavily, although it could be interpreted as showing a certain amount of influence of the exactly similar environment. But this does not take us far enough. The percentage reckoned for criminal brothers is certainly far too small, and for several reasons. The information regarding criminal sibs came chiefly from the prisoners themselves and from general inquiries from their local authorities, not from police authorities. According to our personal experience, such information is quite inadequate. The criminal records which we obtained, without exception in all the twin cases, gave us much more certain material to work on, although even they were not always complete. In the case of the twins we were dealing mostly with old offenders, and not with single mis-demeanours, which, as a matter of fact, count for quite a lot in ordinary prison records. The proportion of criminal brothers of old offenders is considerably higher than the average. Finally, the reduced size of families of the twin pairs is nearly as great as in the case of those ordinary families in which secondary cases occur (7·75 to 7·6). The average of the criminal subjects is much smaller, although it is still very high in comparison with the average of the population, namely, 5·3. This difference weighs also on the side of environment.

The comparison between dizygotic twins and ordinary criminal sibs therefore gave us the following result: *In the case of crime in dizygotics, the similar environment plays only a very small part.*

The material at Straubing Institute gave information about 62 families in which twins were born, in addition to the 36 pairs which were used for the investigation. They do not count for us, either because they were twins of different sexes or because one or both died in infancy. Among the 15 prisoners belonging to the 62 pairs mentioned, the other twin was either of the opposite sex or had died.

At the time of the investigation there were about 3,500 records in the Institute, of which a great number were incomplete because they had not been kept according to the method which has since been introduced. A calculation of the number of twins among the prisoners cannot therefore give us a useful method to determine whether twinning as such predisposes to crime. We can say that in general among adults every 50th to 60th person is a twin. According to our assumptions it would follow that about every 70th prisoner is a twin, and that would mean that to be one is a protection against crime providing our ratios were correct. But as they were almost certainly based on incomplete records, this conclusion is not permissible. In 36 families containing twins and a known number of children, there were 293 births, i.e. 8·1 per family. This would give us an average number of 6·9 children. In comparison with the average size of families in the whole population to-day, that is a very large figure.

There were 60 criminals among the 293 children. If we deduct our subjects we still have 24 criminals in 255 children. Seventy-two of these at least died in infancy, 17 were not yet old enough to be taken into account. That left us for comparison 166 children, of whom about half were female. Thus among 90 children we ought to find about 24 criminals. Every fourth grown-up male, therefore, would come to grips with the law. We reckoned above that in criminal families about every 12th child is a criminal. The difference found is a clear expression for the special danger in the case of monozygotic twins. If we deduct this we get a figure about similar to that found above.

IV

INDIVIDUAL CASES

I am only going to give as much information with regard to the separate groups of twins as is necessary for the aim of the investigation. Emphasis must be placed on the monozygotic pairs, whether they agree or disagree. The latter seem actually more important than the former. A few leading points will do as far as the dizygotic pairs are concerned. But even with regard to the mono-zygotic pairs I can only give a small amount of the enormous material obtained from official documents and the information supplied by the investigators. There is a certain danger in this. It is possible that in selecting the material I may have taken particu-larly what suited my theory, but I think I have avoided this danger. In many cases the criminal records are so illuminating that nothing really needs to be added to them.

For obvious reasons it was impossible to insert photo-graphs in most cases. I have only done so in two instances. The one concerns a pair who will probably not be set free for a good long time to come. In the other case the brothers are at bottom good-natured, decent chaps for whom I would predict a favourable future. They live in such a remote district that probably no one would recognise them and there is therefore no danger that their photographs in this book may do them any harm. I considered it improper to include the pictures of those who live in large cities.

A. Discordant Dizygotics

The individual twins among the pairs I am going to describe now were never taken for one another. In most cases their very extraordinary differences were emphasised, probably because one generally expects twins to look very much alike. In many instances it was said, "One would hardly take them for brothers (or sisters)." In every case one of the pair was sentenced and the other kept clear of the law. We have legal records for all of them. There are three female (1, 2, 9) and fourteen male pairs.

I am only giving the age, profession, and previous sentences of the criminal twins and the record of other criminals found among their sibs.

(1) 17 years old. Reformatory child—sent to reformatory for theft, swindling, etc.

(2) 17 years old. Reformatory child—21 days' detention for giving false name and unlicensed prostitution.

(3) 22 years old. Carpenter—2 detentions (16 days) for begging and infringement of police street regulations, 14 days' imprisonment for wounding. At the age of 20 was stabbed in a brawl. One brother got 3 years' penal servitude for sexual assault.

(4) 20 years. Manservant—5 months' imprisonment for sexual offence.

(5) 27 years. Dealer—last sentence 1 year's imprisonment for repeated swindling, previous sentences include 60 days' imprisonment for gambling, 1 week for swindling, 1 week's detention for vagrancy, 3 weeks' imprisonment for swindling, 1 week's imprisonment for disturbance of domestic peace, 4 weeks for swindling, and 7 months' imprisonment for repeated swindling. Comes of a well-to-do and decent environment. Is the only criminal in a large group.

(6) 45 years. Day labourer—1 year and 3 months' penal

servitude for sexual offence. Another brother sentenced to 8 months for swindling.

(7) 49 years. Dealer—1 year and 6 months' penal servitude for incest. Previous sentences, 10 days' imprisonment for stealing wood, 1 month's imprisonment for insulting behaviour. No one else punished since then.

(8) 42 years. Innkeeper—1 year and 6 months' penal servitude for arson. Previously sentenced to 4 months' imprisonment for causing bodily injury.

(9) 31 years. Midwife—1 year and 9 months' imprisonment for abortion. No relations sentenced.

(10) 27 years. Workman—2 years' imprisonment for breach of the peace. Previous sentence, 8 days for wounding. One brother got detention for infringement of forest laws.

(11) 26 years. Painter—2 years' penal servitude for burglary. Previous sentences. Stole as a child. 9 sentences for theft and swindling, 5 days', 14 days', 3 months', and finally 7 months' imprisonment. Another brother got 1 day's imprisonment for theft.

(12) 28 years. Manservant—2 years' penal servitude for repeated theft. Previous sentences, for theft of goods, theft of money 4 months, 18 months and 4 months' imprisonment. Record probably incomplete. Father spent everything on drink.

(13) 44 years. Workman—3 years' imprisonment for attempted murder. Previous sentences 1 day's imprisonment for swindling, 5 days' detention for begging, 1 day's detention minor offence. Another brother has had several sentences.

(14) 28 years old. Workman—5 years' penal servitude for a serious theft. At least three previous sentences for theft.

(15) 37 years old. Brickmaker—6 years' penal servitude for theft and other crimes, 21 thefts in all. Previous sentences, bringing a false accusation, 9½ months for wounding, 5 months for embezzlement. Comes of a very decent family. In prison he became schizophrenic.[1]

It is worth noting that in at least ten of the fifteen cases the criminal twin was sentenced more than once, some of

[1] Schizophrenia is a form of mental derangement.

them several times. Four of the subjects are still quite
young, so that one must take into account that the other
one of the pair may still be sentenced. But in these four
cases I have detailed information in which the unsentenced
twin is described as quite a different person from the
criminal. In cases Nos. 1 and 2 I would not like to assume
that the second sister will go wrong like her twin. The
twin brother of No. 4 is, according to all accounts, a
good and decent chap. In the case of No. 3 the criminal
brother, who was finally killed in a public brawl, was,
according to all appearances, the exact opposite of the
survivor. The victim was a particularly rough and brutal
fellow who, according to his record, was almost certain
to come to a bad end in a fight. His good-natured, quiet,
and also much stupider brother was hardly likely to get
mixed up in a brawl.

All the other subjects are well over thirty. According
to previous experience it is unlikely that at this age the
other one of the pair would get into trouble with the law.
In every case the other twin is living in perfectly respectable circumstances; in many cases he is particularly well-
off. In Nos. 5 and 13 the brothers are master-mechanics
who have got on well; in Nos. 6, 12, and 14 they are
skilled workers. The same applies to No. 11, in whose
case all informants emphasise that he is particularly
respectable and generally popular. In Nos. 7 and 8 the
brothers are inn-keepers, comfortably off and generally
respected. The brother of No. 10 is married and in good
circumstances. The twin of No. 15 is an official. The
sister of No. 9 is married to a skilled workman.

On the other hand, other brothers were punished,
sometimes heavily, in five cases. In these cases we prob-

ably do not know the worst, as we have to rely on information given by the subjects themselves and obtained from home. According to experience this is generally incomplete. Nevertheless the ratio is definitely higher than that of average criminal material, a fact which makes the clean record of the twin relative particularly impressive. In these families we have to reckon with particularly bad environmental influences, apart from the fact that the occurrence of crime in them might be interpreted as showing particularly strong criminal heredity.

B. THE CONCORDANT DIZYGOTIC PAIRS

(1a) Of the brothers Nord, born in 1887, Georg was first sentenced in 1905 to two days' imprisonment for theft. There followed in 1906, 1907, 1909, and 1910, sentences of five to eighteen days' imprisonment for embezzlement, theft, swindling, and sexual offences. In 1911 Georg got his first long sentence, when he was condemned to fourteen months' imprisonment for renewed and serious theft. Apart from detention for vagrancy, begging, being without identity papers, and giving false information, he had six more fairly heavy sentences for theft and swindling, ranging from one week's close arrest to eighteen months' imprisonment. Eighteen months and one week's imprisonment, three years' penal servitude, five years' loss of civil rights with police supervision, three years' penal servitude, five years' loss of civil rights, and three years' close imprisonment. He served his last recorded sentence in 1925. There is a remark in the records which leads one to assume later crimes. Georg is now abroad, but not in Austria, although he roamed about there for some time.

His particular line was to get himself apprenticed to a skilled workman in order after a few days to steal all the valuable possessions of the other apprentices during their time off. He then disappeared after having very artfully put people off his track. Georg is a miserable physical specimen, although inclined to be fat. He has a stupid expression and is quite dull.

(1b) Johann, his twin brother, is quite a different person, tall and thin, cheerful and temperamental. He is now an office clerk to a local authority, but his previous record is far from clean. He served four months and sixteen days' imprisonment, and five days' detention. This happened in 1911 and 1913. His crimes were theft, five days' detention; theft, four weeks and two days' imprisonment; giving false information as well as swindling and stealing, ten days' imprisonment; repeated thefts and false information, three months and two days. All this happened in one year. Two years later he got two days or a fine of six marks for swindling.

I was unable to find out how he embarked on this series of crimes, which abruptly came to an end. When I went to the town in which Johann works, I decided at the last moment not to pay him a visit in order not to arouse his suspicions. The suggestion of an acquaintance that his fall was due to a temporary loss of mental balance, due to biological causes, is a fairly admissible one. But this is not at all certain. All the other brothers except one are in very good positions. They gave very meagre answers to my careful inquiries. They don't know the twins very well, as they are all much older and left home early. This also was the case with the last available informant, another brother who had gone to the bad and who had served five years for desertion, and finally got three years' penal servitude for theft. The man could not be got at, and even if it had been possible to see him, one could not have trusted his information.

In spite of all gaps the report shows that the Nord twins are very different from one another, even in their criminal actions. One can hardly think of a greater contrast in the class they come from than that between an official, who, in spite of his previous sentences, has been a respectable person for years, and a common vagrant and professional thief.

2. Erich and Heinrich Garkoch, the second pair of concordant dizygotic twins, show certain differences in their social attitude, though these are possibly not so marked as in the previous case. The brothers, now thirty-two years old, come of a very decent family; their father and grandfather, if our information is correct, were minor Civil Servants. We know nothing derogatory about any of their relations. Perhaps the father didn't get on quite as well as his education would have led one to expect. It is more important to note that he died very young of a "stroke". This fact leads one to suspect syphilis, as the two children born before the twins, the first two, died young. The twins themselves were sickly little children, and the photographs of them in boyhood do not contradict the suspicion of syphilis.

Erich, who was born first, was stronger than Heinrich. He was the better scholar and sometimes got very good marks, though Heinrich was not a bad pupil either. They never got on well together. After their military service examination they went to a technical college for five terms. Both served in the field and were promoted

to be Non-commissioned Officers, but did not serve in the
infantry, with its fatigues and dangers. However, Erich
was the stronger. Heinrich once had a slight "nervous
shock" and after that was easily frightened. Neither got
commissions, neither was wounded, and neither received
a pension.

Neither of them was really keen on his job. After the
war Erich started a "technical office", but he never seems
to have done any real business. He was on very bad
terms with his wife, whom he had married during the
war, but never took any steps for a separation. In 1920
he began a love-affair, for, as he told his mother-in-law,
he was all for change in marriage. This was with a cook,
to whom he was formally betrothed in her father's house,
after which he got the whole of her savings and her
complete trousseau out of her and, in addition, got large
sums of money from her father and brother, the total
amounting to about 20,000 marks. It is typical of Erich
that he calmly allowed his wife to use all the articles of
the trousseau of the new "bride". Later, he used his
office, alleged to exist for the development of patents, to
swindle all sorts of inventors out of various sums of
money which they had paid him for the registration and
working out of the patents. Of course, no business was
ever transacted in Erich's office, but he held off his victims
with all sorts of pretexts, some of them of a pretty subtle
nature. His wife played a suspicious rôle in all this,
although she did not place herself within reach of the law.
Finally, he bought a typewriter on the deferred payment
system and immediately raised money on it without being
able to continue his payments. So he was arrested for
giving false information, swindling, and embezzlement,

and was sentenced for the first time in February 1922 to seventeen months' imprisonment. He was not deprived of his civil rights owing to his youth and to the fact that he had spent four years in his country's service. His good conduct while serving his sentence got him three months' remission. He made a good impression on the officials who dealt with his case.

On being let out he did not return to his old business, but took on others of a more "lucrative" character. He became one of the swindlers of the inflation period, and was connected with a bank of bad reputation. He went in for exchange swindles, and more particularly sold mortgage deeds on rye. At the end of 1923 he got a lot of these out of a victim by promising him he could obtain a large sum for them, without, of course, ever paying a penny. Later, he got hold of two more victims in the same way. Erich drew these people on by starting small deals in which he always paid up in order to get them completely into his clutches. In addition, he sold a motor-bicycle that he had not paid for and did not intend to pay for. His behaviour towards those he swindled must have been amazingly self-confident and audacious. The court noted that the accused had a most extraordinarily glib persuasiveness for a person of his education. He could easily dazzle and deceive simple people or those without experience. He was extremely quick-witted, and by means of his intelligence wriggled like an eel out of difficult situations, unpleasant questions, proven contradictions in his statements, and was very clever in covering up the weak points in his declarations.

In giving judgment the court took particular exception to his constant cynical laughter and the lies he had told during his trial. Nevertheless he managed to get his sentence reduced on appeal, owing to the fact that the chief prosecutors ought to have known perfectly well that they were implicated in dirty business and were, in fact, hoping to do well out of it themselves.

During his second spell of imprisonment Erich again behaved well. He did not make a particularly good impression on his supervisors, owing to his endless chatter, the small amount of work he managed to do, and his constant and probably insincere lamentations. They saw through him as a swindler with deceit in his blood. Still, he managed to get various spells of leave, once on the pretext that his mother had had a stroke—she is still alive to-day.

Heinrich, after the war, became contracting clerk to a municipality. He had a shady reputation, but no one could prove anything against him. In 1921, when acting as buyer for his employers, he took away from a counter a portfolio another buyer had left there. The portfolio was found hidden in his house when it was searched for other objects. He got three days' imprisonment in spite of his numerous threadbare excuses, which did not speak well for his character or for his intelligence. During his imprisonment his behaviour was good and he was not punished. He was put on probation. Heinrich is also married. At the present time he is obviously worn out, and like his brother Erich has gone back to his early trade.

Heinrich seems to be of average intelligence, and appears good-natured, a little reserved, somewhat phlegmatic and commonplace. He certainly has not his brother's verbal facility.

There is no doubt that the brothers resemble one another closely in their behaviour and in their characters, although their temperaments are quite different. It is not possible to determine for certain whether they are dizygotics or monozygotics. They are alleged never to have been taken for one another. The resemblance of their portraits as children is very great, and later on still pretty close. Above all, there is a close resemblance between their bodily characteristics. According to investigations they have the same hair, skin, and eye colour. Their physical measurements agree to an astonishing extent. They had the same illnesses in childhood and later on both were ill for a long time. One had rheumatism of the joints, the other suffered from a kidney disease. If we were to take into account the supposition that one or both had hereditary syphilis, the differences between them would agree very well with monozygotism. In view of Heinrich's neurological symptoms, the assumption that this is the case does not seem unjustified. Nevertheless we have classed this case with the dizygotics. Perhaps it really belongs to the uncertain ones.

It is not necessary to emphasise that according to their records there are considerable differences in the criminality of Erich and Heinrich Garkoch. Erich's subtle swindles cannot be compared with Heinrich's one lapse due to opportunity, which only got him a very light sentence. This might be due to the difference in their intelligences. But we cannot be sure of this. Heinrich had a bad reputation in his office, though nothing could be proved against him. If those suspicions were justified he cannot have been so very clumsy. But these are mere guesses. I could not bring myself to ask for closer information from strangers which would have done the man harm, as he now lives in a very small town. Heinrich himself was examined in detail.

C. The Concordant Monozygotic Pairs

In order to give my readers an opportunity to form their own judgment, I shall go into greater detail with reference to the monozygotic twins. But even here I have to keep within narrow limits. So I have decided not to give lengthy accounts of individual observations and to confine my criticism to one or two points only. I shall, however, give the life-histories in greater detail. The emphasis of this part of the book will be placed on them. If my final observations are to be properly understood, this part must be read with care. The duplicate facts in themselves are so remarkable that the individual cases are well worth careful perusal.

1. *Adolf and August Heufelder*

The grandfather and uncle of these brothers were drunkards. Their father did not drink, but he was a bad-tempered man who treated them roughly. At the same time he was serious, quiet, and depressed. Although he was more intelligent than all his colleagues and made more use of his mind, he never knew what to do with himself. In this respect he was quite helpless. He got on well with his wife. Although he was very industrious and always had work, he remained in subordinate posts. Ten children were born, of whom seven lived, and the family were pretty hard up. The mother was a quiet, good, kind, warm-hearted woman, who adored the twins and always took their part against their father. Later on she managed to help them in the courts. On such occasions she did not stick too closely to the truth. She was slow-witted and never went out except for an occasional breath of air in the parks. Her children were devoted to her. She was not a mental case. The father, who was a painter, had gout in later life and in his last six months was occasionally muddle-headed. He died of gout and heart trouble in 1917; the mother died of heart trouble in 1920. Neither of the parents nor the other five brothers and sisters had ever been sentenced. These latter are all slightly nervous people, but have got on in life and are kind to their unfortunate brothers. Once when the mistress, whom the twins shared, missed a period, one of the sisters gave her something to bring it on, but was not punished for doing so. One of the brothers was unjustly suspected of receiving, but it turned out that the real culprit was August and the brother's innocence was established.

Adolph was born one hour earlier than his twin. He was always a little weaker and more delicate. During his schooldays he had pleurisy, and in consequence missed an annual remove. August was the more intelligent and got through school easily, in spite of his laziness. But Adolph in those days was the better boy. He was more "mother's boy", whilst August was always quickly attracted to bad characters. The twins were never really antagonistic to one another, but they were both selfish, excitable, quarrelsome, and could not get on with one another. If they were alone together for a minute there was sure to be a fight. Thus they developed not merely independently, but in opposition to each other. As their resemblance always caused them to be mixed up at school, they were put into separate classes after their first year. The father could never tell one from the other, nor could the grandmother. The only person who always could was their mother. Later on August had a fall which left him with a scar on his chin, by means of which other people were able to tell them apart.

In spite of the poverty of their home and their father's strictness, both the twins have happy memories of their childhood. They were both particularly fond of their mother, but also had a lot of respect for their father and always emphasise his admirable qualities.

As already said, August was always getting into trouble and being punished at school. He was disobedient, smoked, went about with bad comrades, and at last forged a certificate of leave. He never stuck to his trade of house-painter and as early as 1905 became a vagrant. Adolph also once ran away from his master, but the man arranged matters so that he could finish his apprenticeship. He was better at his job, whilst August showed his abilities in other directions.

August got into trouble before he became a vagrant, Adolph before the end of his apprenticeship. August was imprisoned for theft, whilst Adolph got a detention for stealing wood: the brothers had been sent to the forest to collect wood for the winter and had trespassed—Adolph was caught.

The details of their criminal careers were as follows:

At the age of fourteen August got five days' imprisonment for breaking into a building-site with another boy and stealing iron material. When discovered he threw away the sack containing the stolen goods, told various

CRIMINAL RECORDS

Adolph   *August*

1904. Detention for stealing wood, as above. Both sentenced on several occasions for begging. Dates no longer available, except the first on 5/3/05, 2 days' detention.

1906. July, theft (leather apron), 1 week's imprisonment. December, disturbance of domestic peace and theft, 18 days' imprisonment.

1907. October, theft from a shop-window, 1 year's imprisonment.

1909. May, repeated theft, 3 months' imprisonment.

1910–1912. Military service.

1913. Thefts (bicycle, etc.), 5 months' imprisonment, 3 years' loss of civil rights.

1914. At the Front, prisoner of war, condemned to 5 years for theft.

1920. Theft, theft, theft, serious robbery, condemned for these offences to 14 years' penal servitude.

1904. Theft (storehouse), 5 days' detention.

1906. May, theft from his landlord, 1 month's imprisonment.
May, indecency, theft, 6 months and 6 days' imprisonment.
December, disturbance of domestic peace, inclusive sentence, taking into account the two previous sentences, 7 months and 10 days.

1907. March and April, several thefts, for which 6 months 10 days' imprisonment.

1908. Repeated theft (bicycle), 1 year's imprisonment.

1909. December, 3 burglaries, 4 years' imprisonment, 5 years' loss of civil rights.

1914. Theft (butcher's shop), 4 years' penal servitude, 5 years' loss of civil rights, police supervision.

1919. Theft (bicycle), 2 years imprisonment.

1921. Theft, 4 years' imprisonment and 4 years' loss of civil rights.

1926. Receiving stolen goods, 1 years' imprisonment.

1927. Theft, 20 months' imprisonment.

lies, and only confessed when persuaded to do so by his comrade. His parents turned him out of his home after this, so he wandered about, and when he was in Munich lived with a butcher and his wife. He broke into several of their cupboards, chiefly in order to steal linen. At the same time he roamed about with other boys and once spent a night on a building-site, which was the only time he ran up against his twin. It is typical of August that for a time he was the only one of the gang who escaped. In addition to his sentences for theft he got one for breach of domestic peace. Shortly afterwards, when wandering about on the open road with a comrade, he met a little girl of twelve, whom he suddenly attacked on the grounds that she had "laughed cheekily at his 'prison shoes' ". He threw her down, pulled up her skirts, and tore a little necklace off her neck. (Accidentally?) When his pal protested he let go of the struggling girl, but then with the other went and pawned the necklace for a pot of beer. He was caught in a low Munich public-house. At first he only admitted the theft and declared that it was merely by accident that he had pulled up the girl's skirts. He feared, however, to be accused of rape, so he changed his line and pleaded guilty to a sexual offence against her. After his discharge from prison (seven months) he was arrested for begging on the high-road. In 1908 he was suspected of having stolen a bicycle and the court considered him guilty. He himself protested that he had got the bicycle in exchange for a suit, which he had actually fetched from his home at the time in question. He brought a witness, whose evidence, however, was ruled out because he was a fellow-prisoner August had known when serving an earlier sentence.

AUGUST HEUFELDER

ADOLF HEUFELDER

The State Attorney asked for a sentence of six months, instead of which the court gave him a year. In the following year he was in the worst possible company. With two other very bad characters he broke into summer bungalows in the vicinity of the city, but they did not get anything of much value. They had better luck when they broke into the home of a protector of one of his accomplices, taking several hundred marks from his rifled desk. When caught, August had no money left on him. However, he confessed straightaway to this burglary, although as usual he denied his previous ones. On conviction he admitted them completely. For the whole lot together he got a very heavy sentence, four years' imprisonment, which he served in hospital, as he was seriously ill. The next time he was caught he was practically in rags. Four months after having been let out he broke into a butcher's shop with another fellow and stole quantities of meat and sausages, as well as a little money. Finger-print evidence proved him guilty, but he refused to make a statement. His accomplice declared August was the ringleader, and when it came to his trial he made, as usual, a full confession of his own free-will. For this crime he got four years' penal servitude. He was again seriously ill, but without reforming in consequence. He had to be sent home in custody. In the last days of his imprisonment he made a lot of trouble. He had not had prison punishment for a year previously, probably because he had managed to get himself removed to another institution. While serving his sentence he was forbidden by the local authorities to return home, but had to be taken back there because no one knew what else to do with him. After getting home he met all efforts

E

to turn him out, as well as various detentions, with
passive resistance, always sending his mother to plead on
his behalf. For the first time in his life he worked hard,
earned well, and improved his knowledge in various
directions. The Revolution upset his regular existence.
He belonged to the Red Army, but did not commit any
deeds of violence; nothing could be proved against him
although he had been carefully watched; but he probably
saw to it that his police record disappeared. In June 1919
he was in trouble again. He stole a bicycle in a busy
street and rode away on it, but was knocked off by an
enterprising passer-by. After threatening his pursuer he
escaped. He was caught because in falling off the bicycle
he had dropped his pocket-book. He denied everything
and declared that he had given his pocket-book to someone else to have his workman's card stamped, but in
court he confessed as usual. He served two years for this.
With two others he then carried out a well-planned and
successfully executed theft in the wardrobe-rooms of
a theatre. His younger brother was suspected, almost
certainly unjustly, of receiving the goods. Whereupon
August protested, but declared he would only make a
statement if his brother were completely exonerated.
He refused to give the names of his accomplices. On one
occasion he could not be understood as he had toothache.
Again he confessed at his trial, at which he got four
years' imprisonment. On being discharged he tried to go
straight and lived ex eedingly economically, but looked
in vain for work. After seven months he was again had
up for receiving. He had offered and sold dress materials,
which he had got from a burglarious friend, for far less
than their true value. At that time no other crimes could

be brought home to him. Finally, he was found as an habitual frequenter in the lowest dens. After he served his sentence in June 1927 the old game started all over again; he tried in vain to get work, lived with an old convict who over-charged him, met another professional criminal as badly off as himself, and with him began another series of small burglaries. They broke into several shops without much luck. His accomplice got caught. Investigation revealed August's terrible plight. His rent swallowed all his allowances, he simply could not get work because he had no insurance card and his hands were not those of a workman. He was either dismissed from his job or quickly shown up. Back he went to prison for twenty months. This man, now thirty-eight years of age, has since his fourteenth year spent seventeen years and ten months behind prison bars—sixteen years since the age of twenty. In the last eighteen years he has never had two whole years of freedom.

Adolph was not a good scholar either, but he was a better boy than his brother and managed to keep out of prison for a few years longer, apart from the detention he got at the age of fourteen for stealing wood. He finished his apprenticeship with a master-painter, although he once ran away from him. But at sixteen he was already mixed up in two criminal prosecutions. He and another bad fellow began stealing things of little value whenever they got the chance. When caught he denied it all vigorously and showed his hand by complaining of his treatment during detention. He got one week's imprisonment, to run concurrently with the sentence for breaking of domestic peace mentioned in August's record. After August had been forbidden his home, Adolph got a whole

series of sentences for begging. Finally, he was heavily
sentenced to one year's imprisonment for having acted as
look-out during a big warehouse robbery. In this case he
was again working with the accomplice of his first theft,
with whom he had also been in prison. The affair had
been planned in a low haunt which August also frequented at other times. Adolph, who had taken to
vagrancy at the end of his apprenticeship, went off again
when he was set free. Before doing so, however, he had
got himself three months' imprisonment for stealing
wood; a reversionary theft—the State Attorney himself
protested against the prosecution but was resisted by
the forest administration. Adolph's sentence was the
lightest allowed by law. He worked for a time steadily in
Switzerland, whence he was recalled for military service.
He himself says this was the happiest period of his life.
His captain was a sensible man who did not let his
record count against him. No serious trouble occurred,
although he got eighteen days' C.B. for behaviour "necessary to every decent soldier". Very soon after his military
service Adolph obtained good and steady work. But
after a few months he was mixed up in a series of
suspicious situations. He was alleged to have stolen a
large number of bicycles as well as money, paint, and
moulds from his workshop. Adolph was particularly
good at inventing all sorts of tales, and very cleverly had
managed to pave the way so that his mother could make
exonerating statements on his behalf with a good conscience. In consequence his various crimes only landed
him with a five months' sentence for stealing one
bicycle. At that time Adolph had to pay up under a
paternity order made against him. In spite of this he

lived well, especially on Sundays, and spent a lot of money. But it must be admitted that he worked hard, and outside his employment did jobs on his own. After serving the last sentence he went back to Switzerland and did not return to Germany until the war broke out, in spite of magnificent offers, according to him. He was very soon at the Front, and after a few weeks was slightly wounded and taken prisoner by the French. It was suspected that this was not altogether against his will. He had a bad time in the prison camp. When trying to escape he stole a chicken and an overcoat (was that all?), and was recaptured, heavily punished, and sent to Morocco. It was only a good deal later that his circumstances improved and he became an orderly in an officers' prison camp. Nothing definite can be learnt about this period because Adolph himself was our only informant. An officer with whom he claimed to have been imprisoned could not remember him when questioned. Adolph claims to have tried to escape on many occasions and to have saved a child's life. It is certain that after the war he did escape from imprisonment. He could not settle down to work. At first he was in hospital for a long time. On being discharged he got several heavy sentences in a very short time. One of his exploits, which is proved in the records, was quite a pretty one. In order to get off an old fellow-prisoner, who was being detained on remand, he committed a station theft. The other fellow was, in fact, mistakenly released. Adolph had carefully "lost" an overcoat containing prepared letters in the carriage which he robbed. At this time he was having an affair with August's mistress, as his twin was in prison. He planned a great robbery at the house where she was in service, in

which he was helped by an "official" appointed by the
Revolutionary Party, though a former convict. While
serving his sentence it was discovered that he had taken
part in a robbery with violence. This came out through
his own boasting, even to the lady he had previously
robbed, of his experiences as a prisoner of war. With
another hopeless criminal he had attacked a lonely woman
and cruelly ill-treated and threatened her until she
revealed where her money was hidden. The booty was
very small, but the sentence of fourteen years' penal
servitude was a very heavy one. He is at present serving
it. It could not, however, be proved that he had taken
part in other robberies which occurred in the same
district at the same time. His possible accomplices in
these affairs have since died. They were old burglars,
one of whom committed suicide after robbery with
murder. Adolph confessed, however, to a further shop
burglary, apart from his railway theft, in which he
claimed to have got away with valuable goods.

Both brothers are professional thieves and burglars,
whose crimes, in so far as we know them, are of a pretty
similar character. We must assume, in view of Adolph's
various confessions in prison, that several of them have
probably not come to light. Both of them began stealing
and housebreaking at a very early age. August's offence
against decency in his seventeenth year may have been
due to puberty, as he informed me that his sexual life
began at about this time. Later he certainly did not repeat
similar brutalities. Both Adolph and August proved
by their elaborate burglaries—Adolph breaking into a
private house, August into a theatre—that they were real
professionals at the game.

Nevertheless there are definite differences. Adolph is apparently the more artful of the two, and goes about his crimes in a more subtle way than August. The latter just takes without much reflection what opportunity sends along, and he commits more than one crime simply because chance puts it in his way. Adolph makes his own opportunities and often prepares an alibi in advance.

The war changed Adolph and made him more brutal, harder, more violent, hypocritical, and anti-social. By that time August had become an old burglar, resigned to his ineluctable destiny as a criminal. It gave him no particular pleasure; he had had enough of it and would have liked to get work. Adolph, on the other hand, had a fine time. In his railway robbery he almost showed a sense of humour (otherwise foreign to him); in his last serious robbery, a cold-blooded, unrestricted vileness. It might not be far wrong to ascribe this to the influence of his long and demoralising war imprisonment.

The brothers differ in their behaviour when arrested and examined during detention. To start with they are similar; both always deny everything and lie obstinately. August invariably refuses at first to make a statement, then gradually ceases to lie, and finally always makes a complete confession in court. He only refuses information when he is shielding someone else, which happened on several occasions. He never gives names nor lets anyone else down—"honour among thieves". On one occasion he obstinately refused all information until his brother, who had been wrongly accused of receiving, was discharged.

Adolph, on the other hand, always denies everything, even when on trial, and only confesses when he is forced

to, though not always even then. He still refuses to
confess to his last robbery. He only accuses himself when
he thinks he can secure a change of prison by doing so,
and get himself an opportunity to escape, although in vain.
It is true that once in 1920 he shielded his mistress and
at the same time got a friend out of trouble to some
extent. He committed the railway theft in order to get
an old fellow-prisoner off, but it was good business, and
afterwards he went and gave the swindle away. He is
not particular about letting down his pals, accuses the
innocent, and tries every dodge to get himself off. August
sometimes flares up and loses control of himself when
brought to judgment, but he never goes as far as Adolph,
who once kept on his hat in court and had to be punished
for this insulting behaviour.

August admits that the police have to do their job,
and is not on bad terms with them—some of them seem
to be well disposed towards him; Adolph hates them and
treats them with insolence.

When undergoing sentence, both are exceptionally
difficult owing to their excitability and their emotional
behaviour. They are both full of grievances, quarrelsome, provocative, and paranoic.

I want first to emphasise the similarities. Both start
rows; August began in 1913 the moment he was put
into a cell for three. A fight started at once. A note in
the records shows that a similar incident had occurred
when he served an earlier sentence. The complete records
no longer exist. In 1926 Adolph had a fight with a fellow-
prisoner with whom he shared a cell, and previously had
started a regular prison brawl, in which he had damaged
his cell, screamed wildly, etc. In 1914 August was known

to tremble with rage, Adolph still does so to-day. Both have had attacks of hysteria, August probably as a schoolboy, Adolph later on.

Both are always complaining of physical ailments which examination fails to reveal. They are never satisfied with their medical treatment. They complain of being incompetently or unfairly treated, get cheeky and disobedient, so that occasionally both have to be reported by the doctor for punishment. They both suffer under detention and get more excitable. They complain of sleeplessness and of subjective symptoms in the chest for which no medical evidence can be found.

Both have to have their letters censored; one letter after another has to be kept back. They constantly express themselves on the same subject in the coarsest manner, and throw about open and veiled accusations, exaggerations, and suspicions. They simply cannot stop it, although they know the letters will not get passed. They just manage to vary their expressions. At the same time their inner troubles grow on them; they are both obviously tormented by them, August especially.

They both argue from the particular to the general. During the war August addressed a comprehensive complaint to the Ministry about the food in the prison camp. Adolph proceeds similarly about the causes of crime and the care of prisoners.

They have in common a paranoic and querulous disposition, paranoic in the narrower sense. August suspected deliberate provocations during his first long sentence. But even before this he believed his own allegation that the girl he had attacked had laughed mockingly at his "prison shoes". In prison he opined that he had been

purposely put in a cell next door to that of a gossiper so
that he could be caught out talking; he declares he is
intentionally put in a particularly bad group and is
deliberately given heavy work. During later detention he
was given work he liked, and then another equally agreeable task, and finally another of which he had nothing to
complain. But all these changes—there must be something
wrong with them.

"These constant changes, this continued new learning,
had another reason. I thought I was in a mad-house
in which people are ranked according to their mental
abilities. This searching and sorting tortured me. I
thought to myself, Why should I be specially favoured
with pleasant work? And then always another job. Then
it occurred to me to ask for a change of job. The warder
replied: 'I haven't anything else.'" Thus he wrote in a
"Plea for Humane Treatment". And it is true that this
did torture him. In the typical paranoic manner he was
always finding secret scorn or undertones that only his
imagination could discover in the kindest words, for
example, those of the doctor. With one trouble and
another his general attitude became more and more
inimical. Yet August knew his own nature. He could not
help reproaching himself. In sleepless nights he worried
and tormented himself and often strikingly expressed his
misery in a few words. He nevertheless maintained that
prisoners were badgered and bullied, and that in addition
to the sentence passed by society, the officials wanted
privately to revenge themselves on him and irritated him
deliberately in order that he should let himself in for
extra prison punishment on top of his sentences.

He claims to speak not merely for himself but for

prisoners in general. He never sticks to one thing or to one event. He hates many an official, but he always admits quite spontaneously that he may have made a mistake. If others suggest it he will not have it. So his attitude more or less resembles the point of view of all prisoners in general. There is nothing exclusively personal about it, nothing of the progressive paranoic in the narrower sense. It is thoughtful, clever, reflective, however ill he may be.

Adolph, too, considers he is badgered and now and then unfairly treated. He suspects derision and mockery and personal hatred. He suffers from a venereal disease and is offended by the least allusion to it, although he himself is always talking about his ailment. Like his brother, he has a general paranoic attitude to everything connected with his sentence. But it does not go very deep and is not incorporated in his personality as a whole. On the other hand, in connection with one particular series of events he had a definite paranoic-querulous reaction which developed in two waves and finally landed him in the mental ward. In the fifth year of his last sentence he considered himself wrongly accused and unfairly treated by a hospital warder. He complained, and when his complaints were rejected he continued to put in one accusation after another against the warder, the hospital, the management, with all manner of distortions and suggestions he himself believed. In turn the management, the State Attorney, the Ministry, a private attorney, the Prisoners' Aid Society, and again the State Attorney, Ministry, etc., were ceaselessly importuned. He got more and more excited; one prison punishment followed another; his paranoic-querulous behaviour developed more and more clearly. Finally, a very sensible attorney, formerly a fellow-soldier, used his personal influence and clever tactics more or less to pacify all these harassed officials. But not for long. Adolph alleged that owing to maltreatment during imprisonment and then through various cures he had lost his teeth. He wanted a new artificial set mounted on a gold plate, but instead was given a rubber one. This set, for which he had to pay away his small prisoner's wages, did not fit. A new wave of querulousness was induced by this. It took exactly the same form, although a little mitigated by a more lenient attitude on the part of the officials. He was moved to another institution and finally into the mental ward, where, in spite of a certain pacification, he went on fussing about his plate. In this case we have a regular pathological paranoic-querulous reaction. In addition to his being wilder than August, we must probably take into account the fact of his lengthier sentence. August was never imprisoned for so long and therefore his emotions did not reach boiling-point as Adolph's did.

Here we have a definite difference in the brothers' behaviour, which cannot, however, be put down exclusively to their personalities. The following will show how similarly they react otherwise:

August was just finishing a fairly long sentence. His clothes had been sent to his mother, who, when asked for others, sent him by mistake those of his brother. During the last few days of his sentence August was nervous and, on the day before his discharge, refused to go to work. He then refused to put on his brother's clothes, got out of hand, and behaved abominably in every way. The wise prison governor was glad to be rid of him, and instead of punishing him simply sent him home in handcuffs in order to protect himself against his threats.

Adolph, at the medical examination before his discharge, was impertinent to the doctor and was given two days' arrest. He threw his bread about. When the warder remonstrated with him, he said, "Perhaps you would like a crumb?" Three days' further arrest. When brought before the governor, he said, "I have known for a long time that here might and not right rules." Result—three more days in the cells. So he managed in the course of two days to get eight days' additional arrest. Probably in the same circumstances August would have acted similarly.

Both brothers, of course, received constant punishments for breach of prison discipline. They played various tricks—had tobacco contrary to the rules, got food on their own, destroyed working material, cheeked officials or libelled them, threatened people and got into fights. It is interesting to observe in August's case how his punishments increased towards the end of his sentences; in 1912, with one more year to run, no punishment; in 1913, three punishments—twenty-two days' close arrest in all. Then the difficulties made in order that he should get transferred, twice in 1917 and again in 1925. Adolph is similar. One punishment in 1921, three in 1922, four in 1923, three in 1924, and nine in 1925 (his fifth year). Total, 108 days of special prison punishment. Soon after he was transferred.

Both brothers sometimes work very well, but this does not generally last long and they take every opportunity to get off work owing to alleged ill-health.

Both often stop work for days at a time for no obvious reason.

Apart from the differences in the development of their paranoia, the greatest differences between them are in their respective attitudes to their environment and in the use they make of their free time. Adolph obviously needs human contacts. He is always holding forth and boasting of his war experiences, he has to get himself noticed and create a stir, however much he is obliged to work himself up in order to achieve it. When he is not talking he is writing endless undisciplined, careless, and hastily composed papers. In this respect he is a complete extrovert. August is quite different. His first long sentence matured him very much. He was brought in contact with the works of Greif, Heine, Goethe, and not only quotes them but often understands them thoroughly—he thinks he has something in common with Tasso. He longs for books and for pictures, and wants to learn languages, economics, and geography. He is very unhappy when he has nothing to think about, and really enjoys literature. His descriptive powers are constantly improving and are unusual for a man of his education and whose possibilities for education are so very limited. It is only when he is excited that he expresses himself similarly to Adolph, who, by the way, also tries to learn languages, but who has obviously no staying-power.

There is no doubt that August is much the cleverer and the more introspective of the two; Adolph is stupider and more superficial.

Their handwriting is very similar and shows equal excitability. As their general behaviour would lead one to expect, Adolph's is speedier.

The first personal impression received on meeting them is that of their striking resemblance. All the obvious characteristics are the same, except that August is more bald than his brother. They have the same unusual functional characteristics, the same plastic use of the hands in illustrating their conversation. They are both equally pale to begin with, gradually colouring up under the excitement of talk, and the increasing rate at which their words tumble out as they get going is most striking. They both complain of the same physical troubles.

August makes a more pleasant impression and is a much more complete personality. There is tragedy in the case of this clever, one might almost say profound, creature, who, as he warms up to his subject, does not attempt to mitigate any of his actions. He admits his own unscrupulousness, but also sees the guilt of society in general. Guilt is a mere word to him; he knows better than to believe in it; for him all is fate and necessity. His description of his most recent experiences before going back to prison was so moving that, in addition to the author, the busy prison doctor simply could not tear himself away from his recital. One cannot help admiring the self-discipline of this very excitable, highly strung, unhappy man. Emotionally each incident that happens to him in the institution affects him as if it were a link in a chain of deliberate pin-pricks; yet he tries to be objective, considers each event separately, thinks over all the possible interpretations, distinguishes between his emotional reactions and his cooler judgment, and whenever he possibly can tries to be guided by the latter. He does not suffer any the less for this and is full of suspicion and bitterness. Even so, he is not without love for his fellow-creatures. His is not a calculating nature.

Adolph is different. At one and the same time he is both tearful and boastful, cold and calculating, full of lies and excuses. He suffers, too, but he does not admit his own guilt. He is always looking for excuses in outward events, injustices, and the bad will of others towards him. He is uncontrolled, irritable, but at the same time wheedling. Probably he was like this as a child but developed these traits further in the course of his life. Adolph only thinks of himself, possibly August does the same, but still August does make allowances for others and for society in general. August will often say "An old burglar", speaking of himself in the third person—Adolph always says "I".

August regards his irresponsibility as the cause of his criminality—"and the rest is silence". He does not go into the question of how his fate caused this irresponsibility gradually to become inevitable. Adolph puts down his lapses and his sentences to the social code, plus injustice, his judges' brutality, and the infamies of the police. He says nothing about himself. Neither blames his parents, although they emphasise their father's severity. Neither regards himself as a natural criminal or even a professional one. Both of them go wrong here. August has deeper insight. According to him his parents were good and respectable people and so are his brothers and sisters; only he and his twin are different. However badly they got on together, however different they may have been in many directions, they are real twins down to the very innate tendencies which caused them to go wrong. "Literally the same", as August wrote to Adolph after a visit from the writer. At the same time one must not overlook the environmental conditions which made it impossible for them to get off the path on which they had embarked.

The records of the brothers Heufelder must, like all the other individual cases, be read as a whole. A summary, even if one only put down the most important points, would have to reiterate all the facts over again. Let us repeat just a very few of them. Physically Adolph and August are as like to one another as two peas in a pod. Mentally, down to one or two details, they are equally similar. Their mental differences are probably due simply to a difference in temperament, a mental speeding up. Adolph is livelier, more restless, less serious, and more extroverted. This accounts for a series of secondary differences. Their characters are almost identical. Both are explosive and excitable, inclined to primitive reactions. They are paranoic and at the same time irresponsible, humourless, and egocentric. Adolph is colder and almost entirely without human fellow-feelings, whereas August is much more inclined to human affections. It is not worth while following out the similarities farther, but it is worth noticing how many differences in their behaviour are due to small differences in character, although the former must be taken in connection with the influence of environmental circumstances. This is particularly the case when we consider August's exceptional development during his first comparatively long sentence. He became quite a different person, without, however, getting rid of his innate tendency to go wrong. Adolph never went through a similar development.

There are definite differences in their criminal careers.

F

They committed their crimes quite independently. Adolph was rougher, but August showed that he also was capable of brutality when he committed a sexual assault as a youth. It is also worth emphasising that according to a note in the records (that does not appear in the list of sentences) he once got a small sentence for wounding.

It is useless to try to ascertain in detail how each of them took to crime. Neither of them was work-shy in the narrower sense; as a rule they worked hard during their periods of liberty. Their brothers and sisters' records show that they were not driven at first by real destitution. Irresponsibility is a mere word. Later on we will deal further with this question.

It is worth noting that after he had been a prisoner of war Adolph revealed much higher degrees of unscrupulousness and brutality. This was probably due to external influences. Do not let us forget, however, that these influences joined up with certain original inclinations in Adolph, as, for example, his cold-bloodedness, which differentiate him from August.

It is worth emphasising the different directions taken by the twins' paranoia which developed while serving their sentences. It gives us a clear picture of temperamental plus environmental influences, such as length of sentences and the respective attitudes of the officials.

The two brothers show us particularly clearly how essentials are definitely decided from within by an inborn law, but how the environment and its various influences shape the same raw material into superficially different personalities.

2. Georg and Ferdinand Meister

These two brothers, now thirty years old, have led fairly varied lives. Their parents separated many years ago, as their father was living with another woman; they were not divorced, however, and the father still supports his wife, although he continues to live with his mistress and is completely under her influence. Their mother is a quiet, kind-hearted woman who has not had an easy time of it. The parents' relations are decent people. One of the mother's sisters had three illegitimate children, although all by the same father. One of the twins' sisters suffers from "nervous attacks".

Ever since they were babies the brothers could not be distinguished from one another. It is still obvious that they are twins. Ferdinand had rickets to a much greater degree than Georg and did not walk until he was 4½ years old. He was always weaker and more delicate. The slight differences in pigmentation between them may be due to the different degrees of their ricketiness as children. The twins resemble one another so closely in a whole series of striking characteristics, including their finger-prints, that there can be no doubt of their monozygotism.

Ferdinand is the elder by two hours. They grew up together and had whooping-cough, measles, and scarlet fever at one and the same time. Georg had pneumonia at the age of five; Ferdinand suffered from laryngitis when he was ill. In 1916, when living several hundred kilometres apart, both suddenly and without any pre-monitory symptoms developed acute appendicitis and had to be operated on at almost the same moment. They both served their first heavy sentences apart from one another at practically the same time. They were not naughty children and got on well together. Probably on account of his long illness in babyhood, Ferdinand was always the more selfish of the two. Georg gladly gave way to him. They were mostly together at school and did their lessons about equally well. Ferdinand was a little better at arithmetic, Georg at history. Both were good at gymnastics, one a little better at drawing, the other at music. Both showed a good deal of imagination in essay-writing and other directions. They are still keen readers and have a very similar taste in literature. Ferdinand was more of a chatterer and Georg took more easily to fighting, often defending his weaker twin. Puberty came to them at the same period and both masturbated for a short time. Later on Ferdinand, who was a waiter, had rather more affairs with women than Georg.

At puberty both were attacked by wanderlust. Georg ran away from home on several occasions, a warrant was issued for him, and he could not keep his job anywhere. Ferdinand also decamped from his apprenticeship and managed to satisfy his desire to travel by becoming a ship's boy. Both boys ran away for the first time from places which were about 200 kilometres apart; both quite independently of one another but at exactly the same time. Neither of them cared much for work and took to all sorts of jobs. Finally, Ferdinand became a waiter, while Georg was a wood-worker, although he never properly finished his apprenticeship.

Both volunteered for active service. Ferdinand was in the Navy and Georg first of all at a training school for Non-commissioned Officers. He was dismissed from it because he once mutinied and was given twenty-one days' close arrest. After that and until the end of the war both were in the field as infantrymen. Ferdinand was not wounded. Georg was wounded and also gassed on one occasion. As a result of having been buried in earth he suffered for a time from some sort of "attacks". They took no active part in the Revolution, although Ferdinand was enrolled in the Red Army against his will. (This is on record.) After the war they still had no use for work. Ferdinand tried harder to obtain jobs, but had not much luck. Neither had come into conflict with the law until then, but in 1919 we find Georg mixed up in two prosecutions. He had got a job as messenger and was given a commission, which he executed more or less properly. But then it occurred to him to return to his old division —he had not yet been discharged, but had gone off without leave—and in order to do so he took a small sum which had been entrusted to him by his master. He got a short sentence. Soon afterwards he stole a bicycle which he saw standing about. For that the Divisional Court locked him up for a couple of months. A year later he was given a detention for wandering about without visible means of support and for begging. He was locked up in a cell with two other prisoners, one of whom, an old convict, incited him to try to escape. First they endeavoured by night to break through the wall of their cell, but in vain. Next morning they attacked the warder, threw a rug over him, and tried to get hold of his keys. His wife arrived on the scene and held them up with a revolver, whereupon all three immediately gave in. Georg thereupon went to penal servitude for a year and behaved blamelessly. A year later he got another small sentence for embezzlement. Since then he has a clean record. At present he is in work.

Ferdinand was not sentenced until later. Just before Georg was punished for mutiny, Ferdinand and a lodger of his mother's broke into an office and took two typewriters, which he pawned or tried to pawn in various towns. In one of these places he got venereal disease from a woman. His delinquency was only discovered a year later because one of his mistresses, with whom he had quarrelled, gave him away. Ferdinand confessed at once, and as his poverty was taken into account as a mitigating circumstance, he was only given a year. Owing to his perfect conduct he only served six months. He has been free since then. In 1926, however, he was seriously suspected of theft and was sacked from one place because, according to a tale he himself told a fellow-patient in hospital, he was caught making a gesture which in Germany stands for stealing.

Both brothers suffered very much during imprisonment; they thought of suicide and were haunted by dreadful phantasies; but, as stated, there were no apparent difficulties.

Since Ferdinand had venereal disease he has become frightened, hypochondriacal, gets melancholy, and only lives for his health. He is always being treated both in and out of hospital for his former recurring gonorrhœa. He is depressed by tales of the dreadful sequels of venereal disease. There are no signs of organic lesions of the nervous system, but he has not been examined by lumbar puncture. Georg worries less. His gonorrhœa was quickly cured, but he also likes to have an occasional rest-cure in hospital.

The brothers Meister show an innate lack of self-control. They are weak-willed and work-shy. Both are afflicted with wanderlust, to which they give way without resistance. Both are irresponsible, but decent enough fellows at heart. They are not positive criminals. Opportunity finds them incapable of resistance, but they only commit serious offences in the company of others and during bad times. If their circumstances improve they will probably stay out of trouble. One of them appears to be a weaker edition of the other. Their reactions to definite situations, as, for example, to prison life, are identical. Ferdinand's reaction to his venereal disease shows up his weaker character.

They put down their criminality to bad luck or rather to destiny. When asked a merely general question (whether they had ever had anything to do with the police) they quite candidly told of their experiences. Both of them get more deeply moved when describing their depression in prison. Both, by the way, are full of gratitude towards their respective prison doctors, who treated them with a great deal of sympathy.

Perhaps they are always finding their way into hospital because of the effect of their prison experiences. They belong to the dregs of whom there is always a goodly proportion in every large hospital—people who are suffering from trivial ailments, often the remnants of an earlier attack of gonorrhœa, and who use them as an excuse to get off work. Among these there are many old convicts. In this way the hospital often becomes an outlet for getting rid of many of the weaker criminal impulses. It would be worth while going into this question at some time or another.

3. *Josef and Wilhelm Rieder.*

Josef and Wilhelm Rieder are now in their 38th year. Until they were ten it was simply impossible to tell them apart; even to-day it is not easy to do so. They are two decent chaps, but it is difficult to get anything out of them. It is hard to get even their mother to answer the most diplomatic questions. Their local After-Care Institute, which practically never fails, could get nothing out of her. Their mother is a friendly, quiet, generally gay and sociable woman, but who nevertheless is fairly suspicious and does not always get on well with her husband and neighbours. After the early death of the twins' father she married a second time. Her husband was a man by whom she had had a child before her first marriage. Their father was not the success he had been expected to be. He was a serious, curt man, who lost a lot of money on "inventions". He had a son by his first marriage, who was not much good and was in an Institution. Thus he had "criminal" children by two different women. Nothing more, nothing derogatory, at any rate, is known of the parents' families, nor about the available brothers and sisters. The boys were well treated by their stepfather.

Their economic circumstances were not bad. Both were healthy children, though Wilhelm was always a bit weaker than Josef. Both were lively, rather quarrelsome, certainly not stupid. They had a Christian and strict education, and were often beaten, according to Wilhelm, because they were regular guttersnipes. They had the same good marks for school work. Both always smoked a lot and liked drinking. They were not merely guttersnipes, but quite early regular "bad lads". They were the terror of their teachers. Their behaviour at school was "simply indescribable". When punished they just grinned ironically. When physically chastised they used to struggle. Their behaviour made them "very dangerous, not only to other scholars, but to the whole district". Before he was fifteen (October 1903) Wilhelm was urged by another boy at Mass to steal a whole lot of small things, and was severely reprimanded for doing so. Shortly afterwards Josef stole a book on how to write love-letters and several steel nibs off a counter. A little later he tried to commit more thefts, for which he got two days' imprisonment (December 1903). The very same day Wilhelm was again sentenced to one day's imprisonment for theft. He and another boy, D., had stolen two rings from a counter-box in a shop, one of which he gave to a girl. He also got one day's detention for taking food-stuffs—he had stolen cigarettes from a barrow. They committed their next crime together and with their friend D. They broke open a cash-box in a shop and took ten marks out of it. They were given the heavy sentence of three weeks' imprisonment, partly owing to the fact, no doubt, that D. committed suicide. After the discovery of their crime D. had told the twins that he was going to kill himself. Josef had answered, "You're right: we will hang ourselves after you." Josef and another boy then watched D. hang himself, but, of course, did not follow suit. Wilhelm went to break the news to D.'s mother. In consequence of this it was decided to apply to have the twins sent to a reformatory. D.'s mother and others alleged that the Rieders had corrupted their boys. The twins' mother, their guardian, and priest were all in favour of this plan. The report on this contains allusions to material damage done by them and to anti-social behaviour, and it is also said that before they were old enough to be sentenced the suggestion that they should be sent to an institution had been made in their school reports. In addition to the crimes already mentioned, a whole series of other delinquencies by them both were listed: bathing in forbidden places, trespassing, and several thefts from fields. They were stated to be "very bright lads" who knew perfectly well that they were doing wrong, but who were wild, cheeky, undisciplined, and going straight ahead on the road to ruin.

However, there was no room for them in any available reformatory. At first they stayed with their mother and suddenly behaved themselves properly—apparently their friend's suicide had made a deep impression on them. Wilhelm was apprenticed to a painter, Josef got work in a village at first and later in a factory. Both were at this time hard-working, obedient, and of good conduct, and went regularly to their school continuation classes, where they also behaved faultlessly. Wilhelm was obviously repentant and their teacher thought he was the better of the two. He urged that the boys should be separated. This was quite unnecessary, for they both wanted to get out into the world. In October 1904 Josef disappeared for three weeks and was finally taken up by a policeman. In 1906 Wilhelm ran away from his master and was detained for vagrancy one hundred kilometres away. There were, however, no further prosecutions. After June 1906 Josef was no longer reported as in work, nor was Wilhelm from November 1907. The latter was travelling about, whilst the former spent a year and a half in a coachman's job in another part of Germany. Their conduct was good, and in November 1908 they were no longer under official supervision.

Wilhelm had become a painter and continued to live with his mother. He managed to keep out of jail for more than ten years. Not so Josef, who spent years in distant places and had a lot more "bad luck" before he was twenty. Details are not known. However, a note in the records of his last crime mentions nine previous sentences for theft, receiving, wilful damage, wounding, and begging. Just before his military service Josef turned up as a swing attendant on a fair-ground, where he was in bad company. He and another fellow one night stood 45 litres of beer, which was drunk by five lads, all of them still quite young. The whole amount disappeared by just after midnight, and they were all thoroughly intoxicated. Towards three in the morning the lads were taken to the police station for rowdy singing, but were discharged. They were all drunk, but not incapably so. Off they went again, singing and shouting, tearing down plants from window-boxes, throwing tiles at a board on a scaffolding, finally destroying a lamp-post because they simply had to make a row, and ringing door-bells. Josef was caught by a policeman when using the pavement for an improper purpose. Two of his comrades tried to rescue him and the policeman fired into the air. However, they got hold of his sabre and gave him a knock on the head with a beer mug. Another lad started to throw a barrel they had with them at the unfortunate policeman. But help was at hand; three more officers started to chase the flying lads, who met them armed with stones. The officers then went for them with drawn sabres, wounded

them all, tied them up, and overcame further "resistance"
with cudgels and handcuffs. However, they managed to
break another window or two in the cells and in the
police-waggon. Josef is not mentioned in the list of these
additional delinquencies, but freely admitted that he had
fought back after he had been hit. In fact, he admitted
everything he could remember. Josef's cheery evening
brought him two weeks' detention for disorderly conduct,
one day's detention for breaking police rules, and one
year and three months' imprisonment for resisting the
officers. His prison record was unfortunately destroyed,
but apparently he behaved himself quite well. And this
was the end of his official criminal career. He married a
very respectable woman, by whom he had a son. He
went through the whole of the war and for many years
has been in good employment, though not at his old job.

Wilhelm, on the other hand, was at first quite respectable. He worked hard, served his military term, and
married early, but lost his excellent wife in her first
confinement. He had a healthy child by this marriage
and for its sake very soon married again. The woman had
already been divorced and was, as we say, a regular
"pair of pincers", who made his life a burden to him.
However, he soon went to the Front, so at first things
were not too bad. All went well at the start and he got
on with his superiors. In 1916, however, he was "buried",
and as a result suffered from nervous troubles, trembling
"attacks", and was finally discharged with a pension for
tuberculosis of the lungs caught on active service.

That settled his fate. His wife led him a hard life and
he consoled himself with a nice young girl, a waitress.
The girl's mother thought she must be crazy to give up

a good job to go about with a "bad lot" like Wilhelm and have children by him. But really it was the other way round. The girl's brother was a bad character, but she herself was a good-natured, cheerful, light-hearted, and faithful creature, who was very fond of Wilhelm and lied magnificently for him. Nevertheless Wilhelm was now in rather dubious company. He gave up a good job and became a dealer and profiteer on a large, and by no means admirable, scale. His colleagues were caught at it; Wilhelm was accused by his own angry wife. The result was the first sentence of a new series—three months' imprisonment for unauthorised trading in food-stuffs, etc. The second sentence, again got him by his revengeful wife, was three months for desertion. After the divorce Wilhelm married his mistress, by whom he had had several illegitimate children. Under her influence he became a Protestant. He could not get on with work; trading was much easier, and so in 1920 he got another sentence for continued unauthorised deals. The records of this occasion give a good picture of the set Wilhelm had got into. Profiteers, prostitutes, thieves—a bad lot. Of them all Wilhelm was the best-natured and most harmless, and his new wife was similar. The following year he and a couple of others tried to steal flour; they did not succeed, but took instead a couple of driving-belts and were caught trying to get rid of their spoils in a low den. This theft, which was apparently committed under fairly great stress, led to four months' imprisonment. In 1923 Wilhelm, having gone shopping before a visit to his children (who were in a home), took a bicycle away with him. It was a lady's bicycle and he was caught when trying to exchange it. His beloved lied most mar-

vellously and Wilhelm had only to follow her lead. But
he was nevertheless sentenced to six weeks' imprisonment. At the end of the very same year he sold a bicycle,
which had been stolen from his home town, in another
place. When he noticed the buyer's suspicions he tried
to escape arrest, but in vain; and on a third and very
similar occasion his wordy excuses only got him six
months for embezzlement. Two years later he went off
again with a bicycle he had found when "looking for
work" a long way off. Although great care was taken and
the bicycle was passed on to three more people, including
his brother-in-law, and was pawned by a fourth, with a
fifth as witness, the story got out and Wilhelm went to
jail for a further six months. Since then he has not been
caught again and appears to have found work.

Wilhelm's prison conduct was always good, except that
he was once caught talking during forbidden hours. He
was willing and industrious and did not make a bad
impression on those who had to deal with him, although
he was not really trusted. It was noticed by all that he
was a good-tempered creature, obviously suggestible and
weak. In later years he had drunk heavily and could
probably be described as a "thoughtless drinker". In
addition his consumption kept on breaking out.

It is quite obvious that he was no more able to get out
of the set his new wife had brought him into than Josef
was able to free himself from the bad boys whom he
associated with in his twenties. The wife herself was undoubtedly good-natured, but she needed money. During
the summer Wilhelm worked very hard, but in winter
there is nothing much for painters to do, and they were
always short of cash. Wilhelm was mostly in prison in

winter. His wife was always getting his sentences postponed and tried in every way to help him and obtain
favours for him, but was never quarrelsome about it.
When her husband was in prison she managed to get on
without him. She took in prostitutes, sometimes even
when he was at home. In 1926 two prostitutes lived for a
year in Wilhelm's house, paying ten marks a week for their
board and lodging. As early as 1923 circumstances were
bad; they had prostitutes as lodgers, who brought men
back with them, as well as a young lady who was
being kept by her lover. Once a policeman found two
couples in a room, one young lady undressed, the other
on the divan with her lover, as well as Wilhelm, drunk
after a heavy night. He was several times accused of
procuring. In addition Wilhelm and his last wife had
trouble for many years on account of their liaison, which
got them several sentences for concubinage until they
could at last get married. She was once in conflict with the
law for breaking the peace.

Josef only reappeared on the scene once more (on the
occasion of a deal in food-stuffs) in a shadowy way—so
closely resembling his brother that their identities were con-
fused. Unfortunately the court did not follow the matter up.

The brothers Rieder are obviously very similar, good-
natured, weak, suggestible creatures, with a liking for
drink and open to all external influences. They are not
active evil-doers, quite the contrary. Provided they have
some outward support there is no danger of them going
off the rails, although it cannot change their natures.
As soon as they get into bad company they fall without
resistance for the worst influences. Their chief innate
characteristic is their suggestibility, and this also is at

the bottom of their criminality. They are typical exogenous "criminals", owing to their inner tendencies, which they cannot get rid of. In other economic circumstances they would probably go a good deal straighter than they do. One might just as well say their inborn tendencies are to blame, as the contrary. Both would be right and wrong. Heredity is nothing without environment.

Environment plays an important part here with respect to alcohol—this poison breaks down even further their existing inability to resist temptation. At the same time it would be incorrect to assert that without the poison they would not have gone wrong.

Their extreme suggestibility also determines their attitude to crime. Josef seems to have become stronger under the influence of his energetic wife. Wilhelm, however, had the misfortune to lose his first good wife and to have his home made unbearable for him by the second one's bad temper. This drove him to drink and into the arms of another woman, who, although she herself was nice and good-natured, was mixed up with a bad set and only saw harm in her husband's criminality in so far as he occasionally let himself get caught.

4. Wolfgang and Herbert Lauterbach

Wolfgang	Herbert
Crime: Swindling on three occasions and continually producing false information of a grave character, together with further attempted or successful swindles. First sentence in 1924, 5 years' imprisonment; second sentence in 1925, 4 years and 3 months' imprisonment.	Crime: Seven cases of swindling. Sentences: 1926, first sentence of 4 years and 8 months' imprisonment with 5 years' loss of civil rights, on the first count; on the second count, 3 years and 6 months' imprisonment with 5 years' loss of civil rights.

Neither had been previously sentenced. Their early history is fairly obscure, as their stories are not only mutually inconsistent but full of contradictions as well. The investigating judges had the greatest difficulties in ascertaining a few facts, and only managed to do so successfully with regard to small details. Most of the story remains hidden in obscurity, and let us emphasise the point at the start—both brothers were always lucky enough to get the courts to accept the version most favourable to themselves, and, what is more, quite independently. One of them was tried in a large Prussian city, the other in Bavaria. In prison also they were similarly treated to an astonishing degree; although one was in Prussia and the other in Bavaria, both managed to obtain very considerable concessions, including occasional leave of absence from prison. In what follows I shall simply state what is definitely known and endeavour to clear up what is obscure.

Their grandfather was an innkeeper. Their father died some years ago of cancer of the kidneys; according to Herbert, he drank, but was an energetic, enterprising, good, and serious man, who was respected. Various accounts state that he was a business man, a factory owner, or director of a large concern. In reality he was probably a small man of business. According to reliable information obtained elsewhere, the mother was a woman of little education and had been a housekeeper. She is also alleged to have been fond of drink and was apparently excitable, moody, temperamental, very keen on pleasure, fond of taking medicines of all kinds, and hysterical. (According to Herbert.) Occasionally she accompanied her sons on their "business journeys", lived extravagantly in their company, and made herself useful to them. One informant states that her conversation was as imaginative as that of her sons. But it is unlikely that she played an active part in their transactions. The only other and younger brother appears to be weak-willed and of little intelligence, but not a swindler. He is divorced and, according to the records, has taken to one profession after another.

The twins are alleged seven-months' babies. They were very weakly and were kept in an incubator as infants. They developed very slowly until their thirteenth year, then normally. Their resemblance as children was very great and their own mother could only tell them apart by their freckles. At school, too, they were often mixed up and used to be caned for one another's misdeeds. Later on Herbert became rather taller and slimmer (168 cm.). Wolfgang was stronger and shorter (167 cm.). To-day their resemblance is extraordinary, and their records emphasise the fact that they were taken for one another. Their voices are identical. Wolfgang has somewhat larger hands and feet. His shoe number is 42, Herbert's 41. Morphologically their faces are quite similar, although Wolfgang's expression is colder and more determined than Herbert's. Their characters, eye-colour, shape, growth, and parting of hair, etc., are identical. Their finger-prints are, roughly speaking, mirror images of one another. The twins had all the usual children's ailments. Herbert had diphtheria particularly badly, and traces his greater weakliness, together with paralysis of the vocal cords, from which he suffered from five to seven, and fainting fits, which he had from six to thirteen, back to it. They were the best gymnasts at school, but otherwise not much good there.

Wolfgang declares that he first went to a High School and from there to a more advanced one in order to pass the examination qualifying him for one year's military service, but the latter school obviously never existed. Herbert claims to have reached the Upper Third Form in the High School, but according to the results of inquiries made he only managed to get as far as a much lower form. He could bring no evidence to support his statement that he passed his one year's service examination during the war. Wolfgang served of his own accord, but not in the higher class, because, he said, he had not the means to do so. Herbert was not called up because he was physically unfit. Wolfgang had chosen a technical profession and spent a couple of terms at a private technical institute. According to him he passed various examinations, but this cannot be proved. Herbert became a commercial clerk, apparently with good prospects.

War Records.—Wolfgang never served at the Front. He was working before and during the war on his invention, the alleged future value of which got him a "dug-out" job in the employment of a municipality. He was not promoted to officer's rank. However, his wife's photograph appeared in an illustrated journal as that of the wife of Captain von Lauterbach. Apparently Wolfgang was ill for a long time during the war, but there are no pension papers. Wolfgang does not boast of military exploits, but he suddenly ennobled himself, and finally gave himself the title of Baron. His father is alleged to have told him that the family was originally a noble one, but had dropped the title on financial grounds.

Herbert did not call himself "von", but gave further details. According to him, their father dropped his title in 1889 after a controversy with the Ministry. As the Herald's Office (College of Heralds) had stated quite generally that a dropped title which had a secure basis could be resuscitated, Wolfgang simply called himself von Lauterbach. The bases had certainly all vanished except for a Cross of St. John and a signet-ring. The crest on the ring did not agree with that of the baron Wolfgang later became, and the genealogy of the family he claims to belong to simply never existed at all. In spite of all this the court refused to decide whether Wolfgang was entitled to his rank or not and continued to call him Herr von Lauterbach.

As stated, Herbert was not called up. When war was declared he was book-keeper to a large firm. According to himself he made some extremely valuable military inventions, for which he afterwards received an important decoration. The firm states that he was actually a business clerk and cashier. "At his last place he committed gross defalcations in his wages book, and was so careless with the large sums entrusted him for wages that he caused us considerable losses." On that account he left this job and volunteered with the Flying Corps. He claims to have received numerous decorations and to have made 700 flights into enemy territory, to have crashed, and been shot down. Actually he was only at the Front for a few days and reported sick almost immediately. Far from the Front he was given a very generalised report from an officer, whom he ever afterwards cited as a reference, but who by this time had long been dead. A report from other quarters states that he was authorised to act as buyer for the Officers' Mess. Herbert frequented it, much to the astonishment of the officers and gentlemen who attended it. They also wondered why he was never sent to the Front. There are no records of his alleged decorations, nor of pensions, in spite of his alleged skull wounds, epileptical attacks, etc. Later on he had an officer's sword hung up in his flat, although actually he never got beyond non-commissioned rank. After the war he claimed to have saved the lives of two children simultaneously, and to have got the life-saving medal for this heroic deed. The present police authorities and the Ministry of the Interior know nothing whatever about this event. It must be emphasised that in spite of all this, brave conduct at the Front and life-saving were taken into account in his favour when sentence was passed on him.

Marriage and Sexual Life

Apparently Wolfgang was having affairs with women during his military service. He married in 1913 and had three children. Strangers state that his wife was simple, clever, and reserved. Wolfgang was obviously not made for monogamy. Later on he always had remarkably pretty private secretaries. Once he bought a fur coat for a woman he had picked up in a night haunt, but of course paid for it with a bad cheque. Although Herbert denies it, he is alleged by an informant to have had an affair with Wolfgang's children's governess, who afterwards became Mrs. Herbert. Herbert claims to have been in love at the age of twenty with a girl in a distant town, but this did not prevent him from getting gonorrhœa twice before the war. He was divorced from his first wife, whom he married in 1914. Once

Herbert declared that it was his fault, but on another occasion that it was his wife's. He tells a touching story of his marriage, in which he appears as the generous, forgiving, trusting, devoted husband. Unfortunately each new version differs from the preceding one. A child was born of this marriage and lives with the mother. His second marriage is obviously successful. Herbert's wife also is clever, reserved, and simple.

The Post-War Period and their Crimes

For some time Wolfgang had been busy with an invention. Although the preliminary ideas were admittedly those of a former employer, he claimed that if he could carry them out they would have importance even for the financial situation of the whole nation. Now according to expert opinion Wolfgang was able to get away with certain easily arranged and impressive demonstrations of his invention which, with the help of various tricks, could easily take in the layman. He had already done this during the war and owed his "dug-out job" to it. Wolfgang got an extraordinary amount of capital out of a constant stream of ignorant folk, bamboozled by the alleged invention, or rather his demonstration of it, together with his splendid appearance, his nobility, and his so-called national importance, to say nothing of his marvellous gift of the gab. Bit by bit he roped in one financier after another, and managed to get together a large capital. Finally, he floated a company, the only assets of which were the invention and the taking of various options on its possible developments, but which distributed numerous shares. The latter came to very high sums in foreign currencies, and Wolfgang sold them in great quantities. Among the large numbers he drew into his net were respected members of pre-war society, as well as factory owners and even technical experts and alleged engineers. By and by financial difficulties arose in spite of the enormous sums which had flowed in. Thereupon another company was started under a still more impressive title, and, as before, Wolfgang was managing director. Although he had given no more demonstrations for years, fresh millions poured into the business. There was only one quite casual demonstration one evening, at the very last moment before the new company was floated. Next morning, when the technical adviser attempted to control the apparatus—Wolfgang had managed to prevent this on the previous evening—the machine resolutely refused to do its bit, in spite of all sorts of precautions. It was alleged that "an enemy or a competitor" must have had a hand in this.

Nevertheless the numbers of the faithful did not diminish. A year after these events Wolfgang put a series of forged dollar cheques into circulation, and then his fate overtook him. In spite of his constant repetition of mysterious tales about Americans who had somehow disappeared and other people who had never existed at all, the legal expert declared positively that Wolfgang was the forger, and the court also held itself competent to judge Wolfgang guilty. It was certain that he had been dealing with members of a forgery gang. It was also certain that he had an accomplice, who was condemned at the same time, who had signed one of the cheques, and who, in the presence of a solicitor, had had curious transactions with him which had no real foundation at all.

Although these forgeries may seem to have been

clumsy and commonplace, Wolfgang's talent for getting
all sorts of intelligent and also critical people to believe
in him for so many years was marvellous. Even to-day,
in spite of his sentences and of several absurd details
which came out during the prosecution and were given
wide publicity, there are still not a few people who
believe in him. Lots of them are convinced of his
genius; they themselves beheld the demonstration, and
their view is that he only refused to go on working at his
apparatus because others were trying to deprive him of
his profits. People who had lost hundreds and thousands
of marks stuck to him at his trial.

At any rate Wolfgang had a good time of it. He had
practically given up work on the apparatus. He always
managed to postpone expert investigation. On one
occasion he had the impertinence to put off an expert
who had travelled a long way to see him by saying he
was due to go for a ride. Once when the apparatus was
going to be examined in an official department, certain
preliminary conditions had not been fulfilled, so the
examination could not take place. Wolfgang managed to
put it off altogether. The technical adviser his company
had provided for him never once saw the thing give any
result, but had been so successfully bamboozled by
Wolfgang that he swore by it and gave the apparatus the
highest praise at a meeting of shareholders. Newspapers
published articles and photographs of the inventor,
loudly proclaiming the fame and importance of the
invention and the patriotism of one who was prepared
to do everything to prevent his creation from falling into
the clutches of the Allies.

Wolfgang did himself well. In 1919 his backers spent

a million marks on a little palace in a large town which had belonged to a Royal prince and which they presented to him. Later on he had a ten-roomed apartment full of valuable furniture and carpets and a staff of servants. One of his brothers was appointed as his secretary; he had several girl secretaries, and at one time a student was appointed as technical assistant, though he never had anything to do. He kept horses and had a deal with an automobile firm; once bought a very expensive motor-car, without paying for it, of course; acquired most valuable furs and clothes for himself, his wife, and mother, paying for them with faked or uncovered cheques. He travelled a great deal and always stayed at the best hotels, where he took a sitting-room as well as bedrooms, and always had a pretty secretary, sometimes also his wife, mother, children, and his brother with him. His office was extremely magnificent. Occasionally he had the brokers in, but more money was always available.

The second sentence states that "the frauds committed by the accused were on such a grand scale that he must be reckoned among the most famous of swindlers".

There is no doubt that the fellow must have had an unusually impressive personality. In spite of having risen from nothing he moved almost exclusively in the best circles. His knowledge was very threadbare and his scientific talk nothing more than empty, half-digested phrases. He was considerably helped also by his colleagues, some of whom repeated his statements in all good faith, and occasionally—as in the case of an irresponsible and bogus former officer—exaggerated them, and thus, according to the court, actively supported the whole swindle. But still Wolfgang was the chief party

to it. He was really inimitable on occasions. Once, for
example, he took a man from whom he had just obtained
a large sum to visit an important bank manager, and in
his presence he declared that next day the bank would
receive half a million in foreign currency on his behalf.
The victim took his word for it and so did the bank
manager, at least at the moment. An experienced technical
business man gave him a lot of money on his statement
that he was short of cash because he had just authorised
a credit of one million marks on his brother's behalf.
He handed him large sums, not once but several times,
as well as his last batch of valuable shares. A big company
gave Wolfgang a cheque with instructions that it should
not be cashed until the following day. The managing
director was afterwards dissatisfied at the cheque having
gone out and tried to have it stopped, only to find that
it had already been cashed. Nevertheless the very same
company soon after provided him with further large
sums. So it went on. Everybody believed in him, and
even the court, although definitely sceptical, believed him
far too much.

After his discharge from the Army, Herbert was first
of all an agent and then started a very dubious export
business. At the time of his brother's crash he also once
gave an uncovered cheque, but was not prosecuted. But
his speciality was to stick to money and securities which
had been entrusted to him by honest folk for investment
overseas. I know two cases of this; one statement was
made under oath, the other seems to me absolutely
genuine. Both would no doubt have got him sentenced
if they had led to prosecution.

Whilst Wolfgang was detained on remand and thousands

still had faith in him, Herbert began to build a similar apparatus, ostensibly to prove the genuineness of his brother's invention. He had previously helped Wolfgang with it, but now he worked according to his own plans, at first using his "private" means, but soon financed by others. One of his victims, whom he deprived of his entire fortune, far more than one hundred thousand marks (gold marks), believes to this very day in Herbert and in his invention. The apparatus is alleged to have worked temporarily, and then again not to have done so. At any rate, it produced nothing; the money had vanished, partly spent on the costs of Wolfgang's trial. Did Herbert believe in Wolfgang's lucky star? He talked of his genius. Nobody can say for certain, not even Herbert himself.

Things went from bad to worse; there was no more money; creditors pressed. And then Herbert made a discovery of his own, a discovery which was in the air. A great scientist stole it from him. As a matter of fact, he also was proved to be wrong. The new invention produced marvels by the simplest means and its value could be immediately demonstrated. Anyone could work the apparatus. When Herbert was there, or if he was working on the apparatus a short time before a demonstration, it always, or nearly always, gave results. If Herbert had not been working on it for some time, nothing happened or else definite results were obtained only very occasionally. Therefore his disappointed audience decided it could not be so simple as all that; there must be some sort of trick about it.

A small employee gave his all; other people of limited means did the same. But now Herbert found a colleague, a clever and wideawake business man, who was much more intelligent than himself but nevertheless believed in him. The State Attorney doubted it, but the court did not, and I myself have no doubts of the man's honest belief in his partner. He now obtained still larger sums, including vast capital from one of Germany's best-known men of affairs. Both partners had debts to pay and the money was soon spent. It was necessary to find more. It is certainly incredible that a man with an excellent reputation in German technical and economic circles should still have believed in Herbert even after what he had seen and investigated for himself. A new company was formed which was to pay out large sums in part-payment, and actually did produce tens of thousands of marks.

Herbert knew as well as Wolfgang how to avoid investigation by independent experts. Either he was unable to be present at the critical moment or else experiments had to be made in his presence immediately before he was about to rush off on a pressing journey. One modest but obstinate investigator, who was well qualified to judge the invention, thought he smelt a rat. He experimented for himself, but without success, and one day he reappeared at Herbert's domicile. On this occasion he proved that the experiments were always negative if Herbert was closely observed, and always positive if he was apparently not being watched. So finally he was shown up, and as there was good evidence of swindling, he was arrested. His little game had lasted for ten whole months.

Herbert also had not done himself badly during this time. He lived in a nice little house, had a manservant in livery, a laboratory assistant, a man secretary, and probably other employees. He also travelled about. His former office in his "export business" had looked like a Minister's reception-room. Now he displayed the same magnificence as his brother Wolfgang. He also lived in first-class hotels, where he always occupied several rooms and appeared with "a suite". He spent several weeks with his family in the most expensive hotel at an expensive watering-place. The poor man had a heart disease and had to have rest or he could not have worked at his invention and its developments! He was so ill that he had to have temporary injections of strophanthin. When in difficulties he had "epileptic" attacks, during which he fell down in the street. If he attempted to repress these attacks his speech centres and his mind were upset, which also prevented him from working. He too allowed himself to be fussed over as a great man, though less obviously. He too was called Herr von Lauterbach or Baron Lauterbach, although he did not write himself down as such in the visitors' books at the hotels. He was alleged to be an officer of the Reserve and to have the Household Order. He dressed well and on several successive occasions, when visiting a creditor, wore a lovely new suit each time. Although he could not pay his rent he asked his landlord for permission to build a garage, as he intended to buy himself a Mercedes car.

On the whole he was less ambitious than Wolfgang. He tried to get rid of people of whom he was tired, as, for example, his loyal helper, with whom he did not want to share the profits and about whom he made nasty remarks. He played one backer off against another, and whenever there was a risk of exposure, telegrams arrived announcing great successes or new offers. He was the more theatrical of the two. The ribbons on his breast stood for seven decorations, and behind him was always the story of the great rescue. Herbert was much more of an idealist than Wolfgang, and so very much more of a decent chap. Wolfgang was always a drinker; of course, there was champagne at Herbert's too, but never to excess.

Both Wolfgang and Herbert always had other business affairs on hand in addition to those described above. Wolfgang had a mine awaiting development and Herbert a marble-works; goodness knows where, far away in a place no one had ever heard of. Large sums could be spent in the form of mortgages on land of little value and already surcharged. All this was done in order to get Wolfgang out of the mess he was in, to pay his debts, and to give him some sort of future on discharge from prison, not to Herbert's own advantage. If any doubts as to the truth of this were raised, Herbert became impudently quarrelsome and emphasised his respectability with a comical self-confidence.

After arrest and before his trial Wolfgang stuck to his assertion that he had made a great discovery. He did all in his power to convince the court of this. While detained for examination he kept on working at his apparatus and assuring everyone that he would be able to produce definite results. He always found new excuses. Finally, he staged a serious illness for himself. His wife smuggled large quantities of drugs into prison for him, which accelerated his pulse. He also faked temperatures and symptomatic pains so that finally the prison doctor, who had at first been extremely critical, became completely bewildered. A medical lecturer was also taken in, and it was only when a professor of surgery was called into consultation that his game was discovered, although, of course, strenuously denied by Wolfgang. He retaliated by accusing the surgeon of prejudice and also of an earlier professional mistake for which he, Wolfgang, had almost paid with his life. Unfortunately the surgeon was unable to remember these early details. At any rate, the incident was concerned with an accident claim for insurance.

Wolfgang never admitted his cheque forgeries. He tried to put all the blame on his accomplices, stuck to his fantastic stories, and always declared that if only he were set free he could show up his enemies and prove his innocence. Once, when he had been on leave, he came back drunk, but otherwise behaved blamelessly.

Herbert.—At first, in spite of all proof to the contrary, Herbert asserted that his invention was genuine. He allowed his experiments to be repeated in a scientific institute. The evidence of several scientists, laboratory assistants, and the foremost detectives of a leading police department, the closest examination of his clothing, and finally an X-ray examination were necessary to force a confession out of him. This was made with enormous moral pathos, which did not accord very well with the fact that in the meanest way he tried to put the blame on his helpers. Whenever he could think up some ridiculous and inadequate accusation against them, he requested permission to make a statement to the examining magistrate. Otherwise he also behaved well and had no objections against the findings of the court. However the examining magistrate had to give him a good talking-to before he could be induced to part with a few articles of value in order to compensate the poorest and most hardly hit of his victims.

Herbert managed to get himself treated by a psychiatrist. During detention he was several times found "unconscious" on the floor by his bed. At the institute where he was sent for observation he was in an hysterical condition.

Appeals.—Wolfgang appealed against his sentence and managed to get it slightly reduced, as in spite of very definite expert evidence the Court of Appeal decided slightly more favourably for his invention than the judge at his trial had done, and also found no evidence of deliberate swindling on two of the lesser counts. The judgment makes enjoyable reading.

Herbert also got his sentence reduced, chiefly because one charge of swindling was disallowed, and one or two other instances were considered in a more favourable light. It is typical of Herbert that he did not try to go back on his confession, but nevertheless allowed it to be understood that his invention was genuine, although not commercially exploitable. As he had been short of money he had to a slight extent endeavoured to anticipate the fortune that was coming to him and had finally exaggerated the merits of his discovery the least little bit. It is really curious to realise that even to-day people not devoid of critical sense do not altogether disbelieve in him.

Imprisonment.—Wolfgang served his term without serious trouble. He behaved unexceptionably, had a pleasant job, and was always putting in petitions for the cancellation of his sentence. At first he invariably emphasised his innocence. It was only after a conference of the officials concerned had decided that a remission of his sentence would nullify the purposes of justice that

Wolfgang suddenly admitted there might have been something in the allegation regarding the cheque swindles. The referee appointed by the court to deal with his applications dismissed a whole sequence of them as frivolous. Wolfgang was at last discharged, although only temporarily. All sorts of wires had been pulled on his behalf, and it is not at all clear how the referee appointed by the court to deal with his case was prevailed upon to change his mind.

Wolfgang got repeated short leaves, and on one occasion he obtained a fairly lengthy one. During some of these his invention again came into play, and new and rather obscure business affairs were started. He always advanced his alleged bad health as a plea for leave. His petitions for this also contained information that can be proved to have been false. It is some time since Wolfgang was finally discharged. My most recent information states that he started once more to work on his apparatus, had a nervous breakdown due to overwork, and went abroad in order to recover from it. He is alleged to have become a morphinomaniac.

While serving his sentence Herbert's behaviour was perfect, and "the sincere, pleasant, modest fellow" won all hearts—rather a joke for those in the know. Herbert did not get such easy work as Wolfgang, and complained to me that he "who had a thousand qualities with which not a hundred prisoners were gifted", had too few opportunities to display them. Herbert also still had his friends, especially the business man whom he had relieved of more than 100,000 marks, and who, nevertheless, still believed in him. Wolfgang's apparatus was assembled in the prison and suddenly gave results which, however, could not be verified by the expert who was immediately called in. Herbert was given leave and at once got feverishly to work in a scientific institute, but without results. There is a lot of mystery connected with this machine. However, large sums again flowed in to back it. Wolfgang's backer once more took a hand in things. When he was obviously about to be caught for further swindling he attempted a ridiculous suicide. Herbert boasted of new inventions. At the same time he had a new series of "attacks" and had got so good at them that, after one crisis, which no one had witnessed, examination actually revealed the Babinski reflex.

According to present information, Herbert is still in prison.

Both brothers wrote a great deal during imprisonment. They produced petition after petition. Wolfgang was always more impudent than Herbert, told more obvious lies, and exaggerated to a greater extent without worrying as to whether his statements were supported by evidence or not. Herbert was always less transparent. He had a certain moral pathos and attempted to create an impression by a lofty manner of speech. He seems to have remained unconscious of the fact that his horrible cold egotism always showed through these beautiful wrappings.

According to himself, Herbert was always more of an "idealist" than Wolfgang. The latter was more unscrupulous, enterprising, keener on pleasure. He was a "strong man", genial, and had the more fantastic imagination. Herbert claims to be more serious, although he admits "the flaw in his character"; he claims to resemble his father, whilst Wolfgang has more in common with their mother. Yet the brothers never developed these contrary affinities. They always got on well, even down to quite small details, although they were separated for a long time and never actually worked together. It is quite certain, at any rate, that they committed their swindles independently of one another. Wolfgang was more interested in practical matters, whilst Herbert was a keen reader, even of the classics. He himself wrote "a book" containing anecdotes of the war. There are alleged to be no differences in most of their peculiarities or in their tastes, as, for example, their preference for particular musical works.

When I met him, Herbert played the part of the social equal. He kept to the prison regulations as if he were doing so out of mere politeness. Incidentally, with a few slight alterations, he tried the same tricks on me that he had played on the prison doctor, his earlier backer, and the High School professors. He had amazing impudence, and on occasion, like all true-born liars, seemed to believe his own stories, although the next minute he would either amend them or profess to believe the contrary, according to his convenience.

Physical examination of Herbert revealed scars on the upper lip and forehead, but no evidence of a skull wound. His blood-pressure was not above normal. Previously the doctor at the watering-place where he had gone for a cure (and other medical men) had diagnosed arteriosclerosis, myocarditis, serious neurasthenia, aneurysm, and so on. His Wassermann test was negative. Actually he has no serious organic lesions, but reveals a number of neurotic symptoms, such as blushing, sudden pallor, perspiration, idiomuscular swellings, palpitations, "exhaustion", etc.

It hardly seems to require further evidence to show that these twins, Wolfgang and Herbert, are as similar in a whole number of basic character traits as one egg is to another. They are both ambitious and at bottom cold and heartless beings, whose rich imagination and astonishing dramatic powers would be hard to beat. They are utterly incapable of truth or loyalty. Their entire behaviour and their conversation are controlled from minute to minute by the ends they have in view and according to their momentary environment. They produce their almost unbelievable stories with the greatest apparent candour.

A certain difference is shown in Wolfgang's greater coarseness and coldness. He takes on more and attempts successfully to mislead large numbers of people at a time. Herbert is less sure of himself and more nervous; he prefers to deal with one victim at a time and does not like to be confronted with several at once, although if necessary he also can tackle them successfully. Herbert calls himself the more "idealistic", but his ideals, if they exist at all, only do so in his mind and not in his will— probably they never go deeper than the tip of his tongue. At bottom Herbert is the cleverer swindler, because, even more thoroughly than his brother, he is able temporarily to believe his own stories, or at any rate to withdraw himself so far from reality that it becomes less concrete to him than his own imaginary pictures. Wolfgang, who is less scrupulous, does not give one this impression; he lacks the quality which in Herbert is always pricking his conscience and forcing him to repress it. He is able to realise the naked truth even while producing lies, and is certainly the more conscious swindler of the two.

There is no doubt at all that both of them have crime in their very blood. Nevertheless it is doubtful whether they could have developed their swindles as fully under other than the special circumstances of the post-war period. Probably not, but their previous history, possibly even before the war, reveals the beginnings of their downfall. The general uncertainty, the desire for money and pleasure which followed the war, the will to believe blindly, and almost the deliberate wish to be bamboozled must have provided most suitable soil for their swindles. So both of them got to work, one of them on his invention, the other on his export business. It was only due to accident that Herbert did not get into the hands of the law at that time—an unfortunate accident, because it sealed the fate of many of his later victims. For Herbert saw the great opportunity which prison had closed to his brilliant brother. Without possessing any previous training, he followed him in his career and made discoveries which were most unwelcome to genuine inventors in the same field. Thus environmental influences determined the form his swindles took, but not the actual tendency to commit them. It is possible that Wolfgang was the leader. But Herbert's career during the war showed plainly that he also was able to satisfy his ambition without serious risks. His whole manner was that of the born swindler, and he had nothing to learn in this respect from his brother. Actually he managed to get himself believed with less trouble than Wolfgang.

We do not know enough of their family history to be able to trace the development of their criminality clearly. It is probably certain that they resembled their mother in their hysterical and slightly pseudological personalities. If we can accept the fact that their father was an energetic person, we might assume that a peculiar heredity caused the brothers to develop their parents' characteristics to a degree that can hardly be called normal. It is a misfortune not only for society but for the individual himself to be born with such a tendency to unreality.

Herbert is physically the weaker and less energetic. He himself attributed this to the serious diphtheria, followed by paralysis, he had suffered from in childhood. General experience does not exclude such a possibility. This might particularly be responsible for his weaker vasomotor system, which conditioned his tendency to fainting and hysterical symptoms similar to fits, as well as his general weakliness. This does not constitute a serious difference between the brothers, but, like all the other differences between them, is merely superficial. It is possible that the more energetic Wolfgang forced the weaker Herbert into following his own type of behaviour; but this would only reveal his weakness in another form, and would not be due to a difference in his own inner being.

5. August and Karl Ostertag

The family of these twins has been going downhill for several generations. One grandfather was a professor in a large university, the other the most respected man in his town. Their father only managed to become a rather unsuccessful business man, and his only brother, an "original", wasted his life uselessly and died probably of a tumour on the brain. The mother's brother died of alcoholic insanity. All three sons went to the bad economically. It was also stated that another branch of the mother's family did not do well. The twins' elder brother had a serious accident in childhood, as a result of which he suffered from fits. He finally died of them, in spite of several unsuccessful operations. Their father was an old man, unnecessarily anxious and weak-willed. At the same time he was obstinate, though completely under the thumb of a housekeeper he employed after the mother's early death from cancer of the breast. The housekeeper obviously decided everything, and it is alleged that she could not bear the twins.

August was the elder and always the stronger of the two. But they were so similar that no one could tell them apart. When they were undergoing their military training in the same company, their similarity and the amusing confusions it led to were the pride of the regiment, and caused them to be specially presented to the local Duke, although they were by no means the best soldiers. Their early development had not been satisfactory to their father. They were never seriously ill, although, apart from children's ailments, they suffered a lot from sore throats. If one was sick their father always made the other put out his tongue, and he was quite right in his assumption that he would get ill also. They did badly at school. August could not get removed from the bottom form, nor Karl from the one above it. They disliked school thoroughly, and once, when they had played truant and were afraid of being punished, they decided it would be best to disappear altogether. Inspired by *Robinson Crusoe* and various robber tales, they planned to go to Africa. August stole 500 marks from his father, but they did not get far. They were caught and sent

to a *pension* in a small town, where they attended a
modern school, which in due course they both
managed to get through at the same time. August
was the leader in all their escapades, but Karl was
always quite willing to take part in them. If, as
children, they had a request to make, August was always
the petitioner. When they left school they went into
different offices in the same business as learners, and,
having finished their course, entered the Army to perform
their one year's service together. In spite of poor quali-
fications both were promoted to be Non-commissioned
Officers at the end of the year. After that they were
employed as clerks with small salaries in different busi-
nesses. When they were twenty-one years old August
proposed to Karl that they should take over the business
in which he was employed and run it on their own.
Karl agreed to this. The price at which they bought it
was far too high, but, in addition, they were both too
ambitious. Several employees were at once engaged,
expensive catalogues were issued, and long journeys were
planned. In addition, both brothers got married, Karl
out of "faithfulness" to his youthful love, although the
girl had just lost the major part of her fortune. While
Karl was on a journey August put Karl's wife's remaining
funds, amounting to a couple of thousand marks, into the
business. In addition, although possibly not on his own,
he got a five-figure sum out of his father, which, with the
knowledge of both brothers, was also swallowed by the
business. When August's fate overtook him, Karl, feeling
himself guilty as well, decamped in fear of proceedings
at the instigation of their father. He wrote him heart-
rending letters, begging him not to deliver him up to

the State Attorney. He threatened to commit suicide if this happened. His father refrained from doing so, but did not forget the affair. Later on August still felt uneasy about the matter and owing to it avoided his father and his home.

While Karl was on a business journey, August, who was in financial difficulties, forged a bill of exchange for quite a large sum. After a few days, however, he gave himself up to the law, as it had not enabled him to get out of his difficulties and he rightly feared early discovery. He got four months' imprisonment for this. At the same time bankruptcy proceedings were begun against them and they lost everything. Karl received the news of his brother's failure by telephone in a distant town and dared not break it to his young wife. He took her to the theatre, but suddenly disappeared in the middle of the performance and rushed blindly off. His wife had to travel a long way after him to bring him back, after the danger of his father's taking action had been removed. August appears to have taken most of the blame on his shoulders in order to protect Karl; the ambitious business had not lasted two years and had swallowed large sums of money.

After this Karl had a hard time making a living in quite small posts. His wife faithfully supported him, and although she herself had rather a difficult character, she tried to put some will-power into the weakling he was. It was characteristic of Karl to get out of a military course for which he was due by having a "fit", which was taken to be epileptical. He had fainted before, on the occasion of a quarrel at his wedding-party. He himself told me with a smile how this military duty was most inopportune; he was in trouble, his wife was alone and at home ill.

His attack set him free of it. Later on such attacks were very useful in getting him out of awkward corners, as, for example, a difficult and worrying post. In addition to these he occasionally resorted to other assistance, such as alcohol, and once drugs. He always had mental troubles of one sort or another.

August also was in subordinate posts, though later on he was rather better off. After his misfortune his first wife had divorced him, so he was free and tried his luck abroad for a time. As, however, he was caught thieving with a business colleague, he was again sentenced to fourteen months' imprisonment, which the Court of Appeal increased to eighteen. He served these and during imprisonment his conduct was good. On his release he went to his brother, who at that time was also out of work. Karl nevertheless took him in and supported him as well as he could. Various common enterprises then followed, but gave either very small results or none at all. Then Karl suddenly had an opportunity to buy a good business under favourable conditions. The working capital was certainly very small, consisting as it did of a little loan from the family. August became his brother's employee, as on account of his sentences he could not take charge in this particular trade himself. In reality, however, he was as good as the owner, signed on Karl's behalf, and was altogether the soul of the business, as he was better versed in this line than his brother was. Karl's wife did not approve of this close connection between them; Karl was only able to keep August by telling her that August got a much lower salary than he really did. In order to hide the truth from her the brothers kept duplicate cash books.

At first everything went very well, business was splendid. Even after his crash Karl could justifiably request his chief creditor not to drop the business as it was a really good one. In the beginning both brothers were well up to it, although Karl, the lazier of the two, worked less than August. But soon things were in an awful mess; neither an opening balance sheet nor yearly accounts were kept and important books were only kept for a couple of months or not at all. In the second year, apart from a few notes, no books were kept at all. In the last months there were no records whatever. In the first year, however, everything went so smoothly and profits were so satisfactory that Karl could meet all his obligations and feel himself quite safe. But at the beginning of the second year he began to lose courage. He had no more grip on affairs and could not acquire it because of the hopeless book-keeping, for which August was responsible. He wavered between hope and hopelessness, his wife and August alternately trying to buck him up. Both brothers stood themselves long summer holidays on the strength of having sold for their own profit goods they had got on commission. Their way of doing this was for one to receive the money without making all the details quite clear to the other, who then did the selling, or else the other way round. It was a ridiculous proceeding and both must have been aware of their guilt, but it obviously satisfied them not to be quite clear as to each other's dealings and to be able to reproach one another should a crisis occur. For some time August had no longer received his salary, but simply took what he wanted from the cash register. It was impossible to keep control of how much he took.

So the crash was bound to come. Karl went off on holiday, then the newly remarried August; immediately afterwards Karl went off again, to be followed once more by his brother. Karl began to get the wind up; he could not get a proper grasp of the situation. He went and fetched his wife to protect him and help him in the business. But one afternoon, when she had gone out to pay a call, Karl lost all hope. He sent money off, took most of the available cash, shut the shop, sent his wife the chief part of the money, and went off vaguely, apparently intending to commit suicide. He had written his brother a postcard saying, "It's all up." First of all he thought he would throw himself in front of a train, and in order to screw up his courage had drunk a bottle of brandy. But even then he could not do it. He had "forgotten" his morphia, which was in the safe, together with a note of warning that it should not be allowed to fall into the wrong hands. He landed in a distant town, but was suddenly moved to return, first by his wife's advertisements for him and then by hearing a hymn and a sermon calling for repentance. His wife received him kindly and took him to the police, who had tried in vain to arrest him on a warrant, but to whom he now gave himself up of his own accord.

August had been arrested some time previously, but had been immediately set free, as he had at first impudently denied all responsibility. At first nothing could be proved against him, chiefly on account of the state of the books. Karl made a more or less voluntary confession, but declared that he had fallen under August's influence, and accused him with regard to various incidents; this, after August had denied all guilt and accused Karl of fast living and telling lies.

It was fairly easy to demonstrate August's guilt to a large extent, although it was pretty certain that Karl was by no means innocent and in several cases was alone responsible. The spirit of the brothers can easily be judged from their hand-in-glove dealings in the case of the goods on commission they had diverted to their own purposes. Their sentences for bankruptcy, for fraud together with embezzlement, and on a further count of embezzlement against Karl, as well as two of the same against August, were severe. Karl got nine months' imprisonment, whilst August received fourteen months' and five years' loss of civil rights. Curiously enough Karl, and only Karl, got the benefit of his psychopathic condition, on account of which his sentence was less heavy. He was put under observation owing to his fits. In consequence of his discharge from the Army he was taken for an epileptic, and at first his wife's information about him was not very clear. August had never had fits. Actually Karl's fits were partly faked, but partly they were typical "hysterical" attacks, with symptoms such as cardiac oppression, breathlessness, and sobbing.

After serving their sentences both brothers lived on a very modest scale. They were never really well off again. Both served in the war, but neither got to the Front. They were either under medical treatment or in hospital for every possible sort of trouble. Karl once gave me a chuckling demonstration of how he had made himself appear sick at his last decisive medical examination.

They have now become stout, settled men, both with enormous bald patches surrounded only by a few stray hairs. Both have rotund fronts, August rather more than Karl. On their photographs they still cannot be properly

distinguished from one another. August has a slight
diabetes mellitus, and Karl is beginning to show symptoms
of the same. Their speech is still so similar that no one
can tell them apart; what is still more curious is that
their very snoring is identical and has the same peculiar
sound. Both are great eaters, who lay more stress on
quantity than quality. Neither smokes and both drink
moderately. Both are excellent hypnotic subjects. In
politics and with regard to art and many other interests
they have the same preferences and opinions. Both like
flowers and the open air, both are unmusical and generally
inartistic. Both are greedy and can never resist taking
what is offered. Both were, and still occasionally are,
depressed and morose, though generally not quite without
reason. They are also excitable and bad-tempered,
hypochondriacal, nervous, cowardly, and neither is quite
truthful. They are easy-going and without real energy.
They always got on admirably together, and even to-day,
after all they have been through together, are still good
friends. They were never jealous of one another.

Still there are important differences between them.
As in childhood, August is still more lively, more energetic
and active, less lazy, though all this, of course, is only
relatively speaking. He is quick of speech, agreeable,
smooth, flattering, gay, and optimistically inclined. Karl,
on the other hand, has to be driven; he is somewhat
pessimistic, at least, occasionally; often grumpy, complaining, out of temper, never or hardly ever amiable, and
talks much less than his brother. He is untidy and does
not bother about his appearance, whereas August is vain—
his vanity being even great enough to overcome his fear
of the dentist. August likes to boast and can lie with

effrontery. Karl is not too particular with the truth, but his divagations are noticeable—he has no talent for lying. August is thoroughly light-hearted, Karl a little heavier in the uptake; August has temperament, Karl is more phlegmatic and limp. In many ways August is decisive, Karl indecisive, and above all easy-going. August is a light lover. He is now married to his third wife, the second having also divorced him, and, as a young man, had five affairs on simultaneously, whilst Karl has stuck as faithfully to his wife as she has to him. She is his mental backbone and provides him with a will. My personal impression of Karl is that he can also make himself pleasant if he wants to. He is a fireside hero, and his people treat him with a lot of kindness mingled with slight contempt. He is not without temperament, at least in conversation. Nevertheless the differences between the brothers are clear and undeniable—that is, if we take *their* inner natures as our measure and not that of the general average.

In examining the bases of the Ostertag twins' criminality, it is somewhat difficult to consider them as criminals at all. They are not, in fact, criminals in the usual meaning of that term: they are good fellows, though insufficiently gifted. It would only have been necessary for fate to have endowed them as well as their uncle, the "original", who was never obliged to work, and they would never have come into conflict with the law. But they came from a home in which they lacked for nothing; they grew up with all sorts of pretensions; their resemblance served them well in the Army, and so long as they were in a protected situation they were more or less all right. But they were unable to support themselves independently in the manner to which they had been accustomed, and even though their demands were not very great they were still too great in proportion to their ability. They were both full of optimism, with ambitious expectations, but so lazy and easy-going that they soon ran out of money, and then, without having any proper grasp of their situation, just muddled along until a crash was inevitable. They tried to avoid it by means of rash transactions which they committed in the hope of being able to make good the eventual loss. But of course they tried in vain, and so they made themselves responsible to the law. Their guilt really consisted in their desire to live well, coupled with their laziness and thoughtlessness, and their lack of courage which made it impossible for them to face facts. They were brought into conflict with the law by traits in common and which lay deep in their inner natures. Although each tried to encourage the other, their attempts to stand on their own feet failed lamentably.

August is certainly the less scrupulous of the two. He also committed a theft, which Karl never did. At the time, of course, he was in special trouble, had to provide for his bride, who was ill, and was without means or assistance from anyone. His difficulties were taken into account by the court, and because of one or two such facts, and largely owing to the good will of his judges, he escaped sentence. Karl was never in a similar position. Nevertheless the question might be asked whether in the other two cases August did not force his weaker-willed brother to do his bidding. In my opinion this did not occur. The court, in deciding that Karl also was definitely to blame, was quite right, and August only got a heavier sentence because he alone happened to have been convicted on a previous occasion. It is, however, hard to believe that Karl would have become a criminal on his own. But August also would not by himself have got into the circumstances he did in Karl's company. Neither of them alone would have had enough courage to take on business activities such as they engaged in together. Their partnership would have been a good thing had they been complementary to one another, but they were far too similar to complement each other. On the contrary, it was the differences in their characters which acted to the detriment of their common enterprises. The greater laziness of one corresponded to the greater carelessness of the other. If one of them on his own could have kept his balance, the two together became so unstable that they could not help going wrong, a fate which in its way is peculiarly tragic.

6. *Ferdinand and Luitpold Schweizer*

These twins, now thirty-three years of age, were separated when eight years old and since then have only met quite occasionally. Their mother, who was as busy as a bee and a bright and good woman, died at this time. She had been seduced by a promise of marriage, but after the twins had been born she had been left in the lurch by her lover, and married someone else later on. When she died the boys were taken in by different families. Their real father is said to have been a respectable workman. The mother's parents were decent folk, but three sons of her sister, i.e. cousins of the twins, all became criminals, one of whom at least was polytropic. Their father and his brother were both drunkards.

Their mother brought them up lovingly and well.
After their separation their fates were not equally favourable. Luitpold was taken in by a family who were fond of
him and with whom he remained for many years, but
Ferdinand was knocked about. However, both were good
scholars and were never seriously ill. When they got to
the continuation schools, which they were attending quite
independently of one another—they lived in different
towns—both were punished for absence without leave.
Ferdinand was reprimanded whereas Luitpold was given
detention.

I will trace their destinies separately. At first Ferdinand
was taken in for three years by a "dealer", and then until
he was fourteen by a peasant. He was treated severely
and without affection by the latter, but the severity was
well deserved. As a result he behaved well at school;
he had very good marks for industry and conduct, and
went to school regularly. He left the peasant to go and
live with his grandmother, who had obviously no influence
on the boy and gave way to him in everything. He
stopped going to school and, as already stated, was
punished for it. He was to have been a baker, but was
apparently not physically strong enough. He was employed in another job as a casual labourer, but as, according to his and his grandmother's opinion, he did not
earn enough in it, he thought it would be much better
to stop work altogether, so he found other things to do.
After having again been reprimanded for being in mischief, he managed, by the time he was sixteen, to have
got mixed up in a whole series of proceedings. His reputation at that early date was already pretty bad; his
teacher stated that the impudent boy had not been to

school for months; he had missed at least 90 per cent. of his time. He vagabonded about. On one occasion, in the company of some other louts, he entered a strange garden and spent several nights in the arbour there. He had found some alcohol there which he set alight, and also a pair of lady's shoes, which he stole, as well as a hammer, which he took in order to knock off their heels for his own use. During the day he made friends with a feeble-minded errand-boy, who was in the habit of sticking to the money given him by his employers' customers. Ferdinand induced him to give him some of this cash, with which he bought himself food. Then he shifted the field of his activities and spent his nights with several young but thoroughly bad lads in a shed belonging to a brewery. One of the gang discovered there a stock of zinc-lined ice-chests. Day by day the gang tore off large portions of the metal, which they pawned at a dealer's. To account for having it in their possession, Ferdinand invented the story that a pig-sty at his home had been demolished. Apart from their stealing they did the most wanton damage to the property of the brewery. Before this was discovered Ferdinand had been caught stealing fruit. Proceedings were taken against him on two occasions, when he was condemned to a sentence of one month and ten days' imprisonment and a fine of 60 marks for his series of crimes, consisting of abetting embezzlement, two thefts, stealing fruit, and trespass.

There is no further mention of Ferdinand in the records for several years. He was employed in various places as day labourer or servant until just after the outbreak of war, when he was conscripted. A few months later he was condemned to five years for desertion. His sentence, however, was postponed, and until the end of the war he served as a dispatch-rider without getting into any further trouble. When the war was over he got among the dealers. He married a far from pleasant woman, by whom he had a son. An official investigation of his position revealed ghastly conditions in Ferdinand's home. One room was stuffed with goods for sale, the other served at one and the same time as kitchen, living-room, and bedroom. He, his wife and child, all lived in it, but were not the only occupants. All sorts of people came to dance, drink, gamble, and to play at forfeit games in which everybody kissed everyone else. Ferdinand was condemned for allowing his wife to misconduct herself in his presence and that of his little boy while he was misbehaving with another female. He told this woman that he had no more use for his wife. However, witnesses agreed that when he discovered her immoral relations he turned the man out of the house. He got one year's penal servitude for aggravated procuring. As soon as he was imprisoned he was condemned to close arrest for having damaged a pair of new shoes by cutting off the uppers. Otherwise his behaviour was quite respectable.

Immediately on his discharge Ferdinand started trading again. He drank, smoked between fifty and sixty cigarettes daily, and had affairs with women, one of whom was divorced and who bore him three illegitimate children. He finally went and lived with her. In the meantime he tried repeatedly to work; once he stood it for five months, but in the end he found work too hard for him. Once he was sacked because he had got a girl into trouble. In 1927 he acted as look-out for a burglar who, he declared, had led him astray. He got four months for this and served them without giving trouble. But on the day of his discharge he was picked up drunk in the street. He returned to his old environment, although he had promised his twin brother to leave his bad company and the town itself. In the meantime he had married his lady-love. At present he is out of work.

On the whole Luitpold got on better. As already stated, during puberty he was punished with detention for missing school. When quite young he was a notably heavy cigarette-smoker. At first he stayed with his adopted father and finished learning his trade. But then he simply vanished into thin air, just at a time when his help was urgently wanted. With the exception of the father, who always took his part and does so still, his adopted family have not a good word for him.

During this time Luitpold was only sentenced once. This boy of 16½ had an affair with a girl who was unfaithful to him. He threatened to do in his rival and lay in wait for him. He, however, came along with a friend and a rope to give Luitpold a good beating. During the struggle Luitpold drew a big, heavy knife and wounded his enemy superficially, but was then beaten almost to pulp by him. The court decided that he had acted in self-defence, though he had gone too far, and he got off with only one week's imprisonment.

Although he was an unstable customer, Luitpold did manage to keep clear of gaol and worked at his job until he was conscripted. He was seriously wounded at the Front, and in 1917 was discharged with a large pension. At that time he married a waitress, by whom he had a child. They were soon divorced. He alleged that he had allowed this because his wife was immoral, and that he often beat her for the same reason. He had taken the blame in the divorce proceedings, though he stated he no longer had a copy of the judgment. The records, however, show that Luitpold spent his very wedding-night, not with his own wife, but with a former mistress! This was not denied. He continued to associate with her and let his master's wife think she was married to him, in order that she should be able to spend the nights in his room with him. After fourteen months the "marriage" was broken off owing to his real wife's complaints.

Ferdinand went one better even than this. Although his first marriage had lasted more than six years, the couple had been separated since his sentence. He was living with at least two women, each one of whom bore him a child. This is in the records of the divorce. He also was divorced on his wife's application.

Some years ago Luitpold married a very energetic woman, who took him firmly in hand. He was only sentenced once more, when he got detention with the option of a fine for a trade misdemeanour. He started a business of his own, but was not able to keep it going. Now he works at his trade and earns regular wages.

However, he is not altogether a reformed character. Let us hear what his present wife has to say, a frank, straightforward person, who knows her own mind. She married him in 1920. At that time he had so utterly gone to pieces that his adopted father had to take him in. He had not a whole pair of trousers to his name. Even to-day he is terribly careless, just like his brother. She does not trust him and insists on keeping her own posses-sions. Marriage has certainly improved him, and he obeys her like a child. "He has no will-power" and does everything she tells him to. She won't allow him to go out by himself. If he gets into bad company here is nothing to be done with him. She insists on his going to church and mission services with her, which he never did before. Whereas he often used to drink twenty-four glasses of beer in a day, now he is forbidden to drink and does not do so. He used to be a passionate gambler: "I got him out of that." He still likes to smoke and gets through about ten cigarettes a day. Here also his wife puts the brakes on him. He cannot keep money. If he has a lot he spends a lot. He dare not go out on his own. He is a fireside hero, but not to her. He is good-natured and soft, generous, and socially agreeable, popular, always cheery and very musical. As a husband he is very considerate. He is so soft that he often cries in church. So the marriage is a success, although his adopted father often warned her not to marry this irresponsible fellow. According to a witness, Luitpold's former wife occasionally visits him, but apparently this does not bother his present one. In view of earlier occurrences it is by no means certain that these visits are quite innocent.

Luitpold has almost nothing to add to his wife's information. He wrote as follows to the doctor about his brother: "I wanted to give him clothes and money and get him a job so that he could have worked hard and led a respectable life. But as I do not agree with boozing and slovenliness nor with laziness, and as he refused to do as I wished, I will have nothing more to do with him in future."

Luitpold was the elder, and probably the more intelligent, though always a little weaker. He still is. Even to-day their resemblance is astonishing. When they were young it was so great that they were always being taken for one another. Even Luitpold's wife knows of cases of this. Their complexion is exactly similar. Their physical measurements show that although Luitpold is taller by 2 cms., he weighs 6 kilograms less than Ferdinand. (Alcohol?) It must be emphasised that Luitpold is both quicker-tempered and sexually less active than Ferdinand. Luitpold's vasomotor system is very unstable; he came back from an interview with his brother weeping and deadly pale. In general he goes pale when excited. Both brothers are very easy to get on with and give information frankly and willingly. To judge by appearances, their behaviour is as strikingly similar as their characters are. This is confirmed unanimously by all informants.

Owing to the death of their mother, the Schweizer twins were separated when eight years old and were brought up in completely different environments. Luitpold found a second home at his adopted father's and master's. Even to-day, in spite of his irresponsibility and ungratefulness, the attitude of the old man towards him is a fatherly one. The kind old fellow is still willing to talk much about the unpleasant incidents in Luitpold's life. Ferdinand was not so lovingly brought up. After the strict system he endured at the trader's, he was transferred to the harsh discipline of a peasant. He soon ran away and planted himself on his grandmother, whose leg he pulled as much as he liked.

Later on the brothers' destinies at first sight seem sufficiently different for one to attribute them to the different educational influences of their childhood. But it is not so simple really, and closer study shows that both were of exactly the same material. Both were completely without will-power and became the creatures of the environment into which they more or less accidentally fell. Their different pasts were possibly partly responsible for their later choice of their companions, but that is as far as the facts would justify one in going. In spite of all differences the similarity of their fates predominates.

It is worth noting that whilst under the strict discipline of his early school years Ferdinand got excellent reports for diligence and conduct. As soon, however, as he got into his grandmother's indulgent care, he started to go wrong. In spite of their completely different circumstances, both brothers were punished during puberty for missing school; Luitpold the more heavily of the two. It is also noteworthy that Ferdinand's conduct while on military service and later in prison was quite satisfactory. He will always behave himself so long as he is subject to severe discipline. The same applies to Luitpold. Although he was irresponsible whilst living with his kind-hearted foster-father, he did not go off the rails; but as soon as he had run away he started to lead a wild life and took to drink and women—just like his brother—he went completely to the dogs. Under the supervision of his second and strong-willed wife, who bosses him as if he were a child, his conduct is completely blameless.

Neither has a "will of his own". When married to their first and most unpleasant wives, under their influence their behaviour was almost incredible. Luitpold's conduct, in spending his wedding-night with another woman, was more than a bit thick, and it would be difficult to find conditions to equal those of Ferdinand's crazy home and marriage. Both are and always were sexually active and unrestrained, and have goodness knows how many illegitimate children; both drink and smoke to excess, unless someone else puts them under strict discipline.

These circumstances do not lead us to put down their different careers, including their criminal activities, exclusively to the educational influences of their childhood. The environmental influences are equally determinative for both; but their personalities remain closely similar.

Ferdinand committed his youthful misdemeanours in bad company. After his desertion his conduct in the field was so good that his sentence was cancelled. Under the influence of his dreadful first wife, then of his mistress, who became his second wife, and who obviously rules him, he remained on their low moral level. But no one knows better than Luitpold's present excellent wife that he also will always be capable of going to the bad.

Luitpold's knifing episode and Ferdinand's destructive behaviour during his early exploits and at the beginning of his imprisonment prove that both brothers are capable of brutality. Nevertheless their lack of self-control goes deeper than this. Superficially there is all the difference in the world between the respectable workman and fireside hero who weeps in church and the rotten fellow who is always being picked up drunk on the street and who goes hawking in the company of a low female. Yet these two contrasted pictures are built up by different outward influences working on the same given material.

The lessons they managed to learn for themselves have little or nothing to do with it. A few years ago the fireside hero of to-day had gone completely to the bad—the burglar's look-out and drunkard was not so long ago, even after he had committed his first misdeed, for many years an upright and untainted soldier.

It is possible that Ferdinand's drunkenness may have damaged him irreparably for the rest of his life. I still think it possible at present that accidental circumstances might reverse the whole picture and that Ferdinand might one day be where Luitpold is now and vice versa.

Such conjectures may be misplaced, but the brothers are being followed up and their life histories will be completed. On the whole it can be said that the Schweizer brothers clearly reveal the influences of environment. However, their conduct is not determined by the environment itself so much as by their innate tendencies, which deliver them both up to whatever may be the stronger influences of the moment, be they good or evil. It seems that in this case also their mental make-up probably remains the decisive factor.

7. *Karl and Ludwig Diener*

The resemblance between these brothers, now twenty-four years old, was always so great that even their parents could only tell them apart by a scar one of them had on his left ear.

Their original environment was a very unfavourable one. Their father was a brutal drunkard, who deserted his family for many years, apparently because he could earn more money at a distance. But after his return he was despised by the whole family for his drunkenness, his

dislike of honest work, and his constant quarrels with
his wife. He is obviously thick-headed, antagonistic to
religion, and in every way a free-thinker. The mother
seems to be a good and decent person, but could not
keep her sons in order. She is also said to be of a nagging
disposition. The eldest brother is twenty years older than
the twins, is a Communist, and drinks like his father, but
has nevertheless got on. During his boyhood he once
got three days' detention for breach of forest law. The
second brother, who for a long time faithfully looked
after the twins, was remarkably industrious, able, respectable, and sober. However, he was killed at the Front in
1916. The family thus lost its principal support. The
next brother, now twenty-eight, is said to be the most
intelligent. Otherwise nothing more is known about
him, except that he was once sentenced to three months
for causing bodily harm. Five other children died young.

The twins were the youngest of the family. Karl was
born first in the normal position, Ludwig half an hour
later with foot presentation. Ludwig is said to have
developed more quickly, and Karl was only able to walk
at two and a half and to talk at three. Both apparently
had convulsions, measles and diphtheria. Karl also had
pneumonia when fourteen years old.

Their upbringing was obviously very inadequate,
especially after the second brother was no longer able to
take care of them. Neither was a good scholar, although
not particularly bad, but their conduct was thoroughly
naughty, and after leaving school, if not before, they
were known as the worst boys of their district. They
certainly worked and paid money at home, but they went
about in bad company, drinking, and, although normally

quite decent chaps, they got quarrelsome and fighting-mad when drunk. Ludwig's first recorded sentence was passed on him when he was eighteen. With a couple of comrades he had stolen half a hundredweight of old iron from a dump, for which he got three days' imprisonment. Both brothers were mixed up in the next crime. One day in the winter of 1924 they emerged rather tight from a public-house, when a snowball hit Ludwig. He started a row and used bad language, especially with reference to a group of men standing by. They came to blows and, after Ludwig had had one on the face, to a wild fight, in which Karl at last drew his knife and wounded one of the attackers on the hand, also stabbing him through the coat in the neighbourhood of his stomach. According to the records, their enemies seem to have been a sad and cowardly lot. Ludwig got two months; Karl, who had in addition insulted and resisted the police, was given four months and one week's imprisonment.

After serving their sentences, during which the behaviour of both was free from blame, Ludwig repented, became more respectable, drank less, and, as previously, had more to do with girls than Karl. Karl declares that, owing to his repentance, Ludwig has now become the exact opposite of himself. Karl went on drinking at least two measures per day, sometimes as many as twelve. He was in the worst possible company. Less than a year after his discharge he was drinking away with a boon companion in various public-houses. His friend, who was heavily drunk, finally started misbehaving in every sort of way, made a row in the street, and smashed things. Karl tried to stop him, and so aroused the other fellow's anger. He was much taller and stronger than Karl, although more completely drunk. He began to ill-treat him, followed him, and once knocked him down. He also knocked down and kicked a passer-by who tried to assist Karl, as well as a female who rushed along to help. Then the tragedy happened. Karl pulled his knife and, as the court decided, stabbed his adversary, without having to do so, as he himself obstinately maintained, in self-defence. His knife went through the skull into the brain, causing an abscess from which the victim died a couple of days later. Karl was sentenced to 2½ years for wounding followed by death. He served his sentence without giving any trouble, and towards the end of it was in the second division. He has now been set free.

In spite of the differences stressed by Karl, the two brothers are extremely similar in all respects. They are both characterised by a certain though not very high degree of irresponsibility, together with abnormal excitability. Like their father and mother, both are addicted to alcohol, which leads them to crimes of alcoholic excitement. It was rather a matter of luck that one of them used his knife. Nevertheless Ludwig seems to have reformed, and it may not be a matter of luck that he was the one who developed better in childhood. He was the second to be born and was lucky enough to have come into the world with foot presentation. This circumstance may be particularly important in the case of twins, owing to the very high risk of damage to the brain in their case.

Innate tendencies combined with the effects of alcohol may have provided the setting for criminality in this case, and the depressing environment may have done the rest. Innate tendencies in themselves were not alone responsible, although the brothers' delinquencies show that they were not without considerable importance. Nevertheless I should like to think that were it not for the evils of drink, which in our country are still inevitable, the two Dieners would not have become criminals.

8. The Brothers Maat

For certain reasons I am unable to go into details in this case. These very similar twins come from an excellent family. They are both extremely "nervous", suffer from neurotic symptoms of the most various kinds, fear neuroses, and disturbances in the nature of fits; one of them occasionally suffers from compulsion neurosis as well. In addition, they reveal various idiosyncrasies, some of them similar, some more or less different. They were very difficult to bring up, and although all sorts of treatments were tried for longer or shorter periods, neither of them did very well. They are now in their middle twenties and it is difficult to imagine that they will ever be of much use. They have been separated for several years.

They are extremely cold, egocentric beings, without any human affections, without sympathy, respect, or affection for their parents or anyone else. They got on badly with one another until after puberty. Then their troubles brought them a little closer together. But their mutual friendliness was due to nothing more than their common interests. Both are extremely anxious for their own safety and callous to anyone else's.

Occasionally, when examining them, it appeared as if one might still discover one or another more or less human affection in them, but it only turned out that at bottom they were both, and had been for a long time, sexual inverts. Both had relations with people of their own sex from puberty onwards, and, as a matter of fact, were kept for as long as he was able to afford it by a homosexual friend. Neither has yet been punished in Germany, but in a foreign country one of them was imprisoned for homosexual activities whilst the other managed to escape arrest just in time. They are an amoral couple, and have both made themselves liable to punishment for the same offence, although actually only one was caught while the other got away.

Mutual influence has certainly no effect on inversion. They spoke with revolting tactlessness and lack of ethical sensibility quite frankly and unashamedly of the most dreadful incidents. But all questions with regard to common sexual experiences, mutual masturbation, common seductions, etc., were answered with emphatic negatives. It was only after each brother had independently recognised his tendencies that they discovered their similarity in this respect and used their common ability to support themselves by their perversity.

Other members of the family do not show the same tendencies, but they do reveal other sexual anomalies. It was not possible to ascertain common experiences at home which could have turned the Maats in the direction of inversion, although the investigator had great knowledge of sexual behaviour and was very well read in the literature. Nowadays one of the brothers seems to be predominantly heterosexual, the other to be bisexual. I need hardly add anything further to this account. It is unquestionable that in this case innate tendencies predominate. It is nevertheless possible that mutual influence was partly responsible for the brothers having transgressed the law. On this point it is impossible to divide up responsibility between heredity and environment.

9. Antonie and Amalie Messer

These twin sisters are now thirty-one years old. They were always extremely alike, and even their husbands occasionally mistook them for one another. They are now stout and jolly women and yet not altogether of a happy disposition. If they have bad luck they are at once deeply affected, become depressed, and contemplate suicide; at any rate, they threaten it. Antonie, who is easily excitable, has on various occasions attempted to kill herself by gas-poisoning, though probably she never seriously intended to do so.

Their father was a very decent man and strict with them; their mother was "too kind". On three occasions she gave birth to twins, but our subjects are the only pair still alive. There are ten other living children, of whom these girls are the sixth and seventh. Their other brothers and sisters were clearly respectable, but the twins only got on well until they left school. They caused a lot of worry even as little children. If they fell or hurt themselves they held their breath and grimaced and gesticulated with their eyes, faces, and hands. They only got over this habit when five years old. "They are only half human", their mother wrote in 1915. Both were quite good scholars, although careless. Finally they ran away from home on several occasions, and when they were sixteen years old it was necessary to apply for them to be put away under compulsory official supervision. "The twins have not yet been sentenced, but are of a very irresponsible disposition.

K

Towards the end of 1912 they ran away from home and at first went into service in M. and F. They soon left, however, wandered about without employment, lived immoral lives, and returned home at the beginning of April, by which time they had quite gone to the bad. On April 27, 1913, they both ran away again and went to L. On April 29th their father fetched them home.

"The very same day both again slipped through their parents' fingers. On May 3, 1913, their father met Amalie at a sweet-stall in M. He had to apply to the police for help before he could get her home. She then had to go into hospital, as she had a venereal disease. Antonie at first served in a sweet-shop in L. and then went into domestic service there. Both twins had frequent pro-miscuous sexual intercourse, and were so far corrupted that their parents were unable to reform them or to protect them. The church, the local orphanage board, and the district authorities recommended official super-vision for both twins. Although they were over sixteen, their immoral lives and their urge to vagrancy gave rise to circumstances which made official supervision impera-tive to avoid their complete ruin." Thus runs the report of the Board for Compulsory Supervision.

In the reformatory Amalie behaved herself, but owing to her excitability Antonie several times got into trouble, was always being sent to different institutions, and once to a clinic for psychiatry. Nevertheless their compulsory education seems to have had some fairly good results in both cases.

After their discharge both of them, although they were now separated, led lives of the most immoral character. Antonie became pregnant, and, in order not to have an illegitimate child, married a man other than her seducer. Some of the later children were her husband's, but she named various men as the fathers of the three or four who came first; among others a brother of her brother-in-law's. Her unhappy marriage, however, continued. The husband was an excitable drunkard, subject to hysterical attacks. He ill-treated his wife and children. Once he pawned the furniture. He quarrelled with his relations. Antonie consoled herself with other men and often left her husband, but nevertheless one must admit she worked as busily as a bee, kept her home clean and looked after her children. In this she was exactly like her twin sister.

Amalie married much later, but in the meantime led the same sort of life as her married sister. She had one lover after another, chiefly foreigners, most of them Frenchmen. She was also kept by a Siamese and was probably unfaithful to them all. Her conduct as a married woman is not very clear. Her husband, a tradesman at present out of a job, who lives on her work, is certainly unfaithful to her. From what we know of her it is unlikely that she is much better than he.

Both sisters had mysterious conflicts with the law. Amalie had an affair with a Frenchman, but claimed not to know he was already married. He finally fled, as a deserter, and a theft was discovered in his lodgings, where Amalie had been.

Amalie was detained for examination and also apparently in order that she might betray the address of the fugitive. Nothing definite, however, could be proved against her. She herself is silent on the point, a bad sign, according to general experience, in her case, for as a rule she only conceals facts which are very much against herself. On the whole she is very chatty and is not too sensitive with regard to delicate matters.

Antonie was served with a warrant, sentencing her to two months' imprisonment for procuring. She accepted it, but this business also is mysterious. Her twin sister had brought her, out of pity, a prostitute, whom she, also out of pity, took in. She discovered too late that the prostitute brought men home, and then threw her out. But the woman had seen too much. She accused her of procuring and also gave information on the anti-marital conditions prevailing in Antonie's home. Antonie only heard of this at the police examination. In order to hide her shame from her husband and to avoid for her children's sake a divorce in which she would be the guilty party, she refused to allow the case to come into court and so had to accept her sentence. In fact, she almost welcomed it, although at times she was strongly depressed, attempted suicide, and worked off her troubles on those who unfortunately had to deal with her. The woman doctor who examined her did not consider her story entirely improbable, although pretty well everything the sisters say should have a question-mark put after it. Since their sentences the twins are no longer friends, as Antonie considers Amalie is to blame for her imprisonment.

It is unnecessary to stress the extreme resemblance of the social behaviour of these twin sisters. A constant sexual urge and lack of self-control decided their destinies, which are only outwardly a little different from one another. Whatever other guilty acts they may commit will be closely allied with their sexual life.

With regard to this pair I have restricted myself to a

few facts only, and have merely mentioned in passing differences in emotional reaction conditioned from without. These do not concern our problem. Were they not sexually entirely without self-control, neither would probably have started to go wrong when still quite young.

Apart from records, medical and educational histories, I am indebted for photographs and very detailed information about the two sisters to Frau Doctor Toni Schmidt-Kraepelin and Fräulein Doctor Emy Motzger, whom I wish to thank sincerely. The twins spoke to both ladies far more frankly than they would probably have done to me.

10. *Georg and Adolf Krämer*

Georg and Adolf, a surprisingly similar pair of lads, are still quite young, not much over twenty. But both have already been sentenced, although for different delinquencies. Their parents' families are well respected at home. Yet the paternal grandfather was a fiery, fierce-tempered, brutal man and the father obviously resembles him. He is silent, unsociable, but very industrious. In his youth he drank a great deal and was several times sentenced for bodily wounding and resistance. Now, however, he is moderate, does not go out much, has not been sentenced for a long time, goes to church, and is good to his family. His sons seem very similar to him, i.e. to the sort of man he was when young. The three eldest—then come the twins—are all hot-tempered and unsociable. One is described as rough, two others as cold-natured, and the last two drink very heavily. All three have been sentenced for bodily wounding, getting respectively eight days, seven weeks, and several lighter sentences, and eight weeks with various lighter sentences. Their misdemeanours always occur under the influence of alcohol. All the brothers are otherwise in good circumstances and have worked well. The mother is a quiet, serious, industrious, good-natured, self-sacrificing, careful woman, who lives solely for her family. She has had ten children and they are all healthy; the younger ones, including another pair of very similar twins, are intelligent and have until now kept out of trouble.

Georg and Adolf, however, are not very bright and both once failed to get moved up because they found lessons difficult. They were brought up together, strictly disciplined, and are still living at home. They did not learn a trade, but worked regularly as day and casual labourers. They gave most of their wages to their parents. They are quiet, slow-moving, and slow-thinking creatures; hardworking, stupid, and monosyllabic, rough diamonds, and, on the whole, still unspoilt. Both are obviously shy, especially Adolf: "When I go through the village and people stare after me I go quite red." Georg also blushes easily, though more when in anger. Both perspire heavily. They are extremely suggestible. In prison Georg could be led by any fellow-prisoner. He had not the courage to answer back or to argue with his fellow-prisoners. All his crimes were committed in the company of others and under the influence of bad friends. On the whole he seems more excitable and sensitive than Adolf. Neither has as yet had anything to do with women.

Their replies to intelligence test questions were extremely sparse. Possibly Georg is a little bit better than Adolf, who is of the opinion that he is perhaps a little brighter than himself. But Georg cannot give up drink.

Adolf only takes three or four glasses once in a while and during the week hardly anything at all, but Georg puts down six to eight glasses regularly, and when drunk becomes excitable and brutal. He is known as a trouble-maker and a fighter, and is badly spoken of in this respect, though not so badly as some others in the place or his older brothers.

Adolf has not yet been sentenced for wounding, but he was punished for stealing. When he was sixteen years old he was sent to fetch beer for the family. Whilst the inn-keeper left the bar, he took a note for a fairly large sum out of the till. His conscience pricked him very soon, he was afraid of discovery, and ran back with the money. He met the innkeeper half-way, and took this person in by pretending to be his own twin brother. "I am not the thief, it was my twin brother Adolf. When he got home father thought he looked so strange. He examined him and found the money in Adolf's pocket. Father has sent me to give it back to you." This was the story Adolf made up. He was sentenced to two days' imprisonmert or a fine of thirty marks. His remark to the doctor that people were astonished that he had not yet been sentenced proves that he can still lie.

But he may have meant that he had not yet been punished for wounding. Georg has already been sentenced three times for this and further proceedings are pending against him. In 1926 he was given respectively eight and fourteen days; in 1927, fifteen days. His present sentence of four months' imprisonment was due to a fairly stupid stabbing affray which occurred after heavy drinking. Two of his brothers and a well-known wielder of the knife were present, but only Georg used his weapon and wounded the other three times, although not heavily. One of the Krämer brothers is said to have started the row.

Adolf was punished for an offence against property, Georg has been sentenced several times for crimes committed when drunk. It should be emphasised that he not only commits these under the influence of alcohol but also in the company of various even more quarrelsome acquaintances. His last offence was against a notorious knifer. It is difficult to imagine such a timid creature doing such things on his own. He needs alcohol and the courage inspired by the company of others in order to be sufficiently aroused to commit deeds of violence.

It is interesting to notice that in spite of their surprisingly similar conduct in general, and their unusual physical resemblance, there are noticeable differences between these twins. Georg drinks more heavily, but that is apparently not due to an inherent difference. In May 1926, before he committed any of his misdeeds, he was hit on the head with a jug and remained unconscious for three hours; he may have sustained more than slight damage to his brain. In view of this a further difference between the brothers arouses still greater interest. Although their height is the same within a few millimetres to Georg's advantage, his measurements from waist to feet are longer by 3·9 cms. than Adolf's, which is a great deal in view of their general height of 165 cms., especially as Adolf's measurement for this part of the body is in itself exceptional. This indicates a certain degree of eunuchoidism, with which one can connect the fact that these two hefty lads have no use at

GEORG KRÄMER

ADOLF KRÄMER

all for girls. The height of the head and neck is much less in Georg than Adolf, namely, 27·3 as against 31·5 cm. This is apparent from the photograph. Adolf's head is also broader by 1 cm.

Georg was eighteen years of age and therefore not yet fully grown when he was hit on the head. The lengthy period of unconsciousness which followed leads one to suspect serious damage to the brain. If one takes into consideration that in such cases there is often slight bleeding at the base of the brain, it is possible to put down the physical differences to this blow. The existing mental differences may be assumed to be closely connected with physical ones. It must at once be admitted that we cannot prove this theory of the case. We have no earlier measurements, and it is indisputable that similar differences between monozygotic twins exist, even without a previous history of injury to the brain. It is also a fact that at the time of the blow Georg was no longer a small boy. The sexual development of both brothers is certainly backward. At the time of his accident Georg was probably going through a critical period. All these facts rather confirm the theory.

Taking the term criminality in its wide sense the behaviour of the Krämer twins agrees; but the nature of their crimes is different. In these circumstances it appears important that not only mental but also physical differences exist between the brothers which might account for the different types of crime committed by them. It appears to be no less significant that the immediate cause of their differences is probably a serious brain injury sustained by Georg at a period of development. It is certainly not accidental that Georg Krämer's brutality keeps on emerging in the guise of alcoholic pugnacity. He has certainly inherited a tendency to it, as a comparison between him, his father, and his brothers proves. The inherited tendencies appear owing to the damage to the brain, whereas in Adolf they have not yet revealed themselves.

Finally, I would like to mention that the physical measurements were taken by my colleague, Dr. Grüber, who was unaware of the point of the investigation. The brothers were also measured separately. Therefore there can be no question of prejudice, quite apart from the fact that my former colleague attributes a good deal more importance to environmental influences than I do.

D. Discordant Identical Pairs

The previous cases have shown us again and again the profound influence of innate tendencies. The following ones, concerning twins whose criminality shows the greatest differences, should give us a complete picture of environmental influences. They will do so, but it will be quite a different picture from what one would have expected. There will be noticeably little evidence in it of influences which exclusively affect the mental faculties.

1. *Otto and Erich Hiersekorn*

These two young men, now twenty-four years old, are trained workmen and good at their jobs. Their family is completely unblemished and also without mental anomalies. Three years ago Otto received a short term of imprisonment for homosexual activities. He has had no other sentences and Erich has never had any trouble with the law. The lives of the brothers have been on the whole uneventful. They have got on well, earned good wages, and live in decent circumstances. Erich has an affair with a respectable girl. Otto, on the other hand, has a deep and jealous "friendship" with a very well educated, exceptionally intelligent, competent, and refined man.

The physical and mental differences between these twins, who were once so similar that no one could tell which was which, are important. At school their teacher requested that they should wear suits of different colours in order that he could distinguish them one from the other. It is still obvious that they are twins, but it is easy to tell them apart. Compared to others they also have many mental qualities in common. But there are also radical differences. First of all, Erich was always definitely the more intelligent. He learnt all subjects excellently, got through school without trouble, and has also exceptional practical ability. He works very regularly at his job. Otto, on the other hand, was slow in the uptake at school and once failed to get removed. His mother took a lot of useless trouble with him; he simply could not learn, especially to do sums. Their differences in character were from the beginning equally emphatic. Erich was serious, straightforward, frank, absolutely truthful, and steady. He always knew what he wanted to do and followed a definite aim. He was satisfied with what he attained. He was slow, but sure, always sensible and matter-of-fact, healthily conscious of his desires and definitely masculine. Perhaps he is a bit of a bore, with all his respectability. He is not particularly excitable nor sensitive, but can be resentful and is determined to get his way. He does not allow himself to be insulted. If that occurs he hits out and knows how to defend himself. Otto was quite different. He was always to the fore in any mischief, just as Erich was in serious affairs; he was always gay, did not mind a bit of leg-pulling, exaggerated, told people tales, and finally came to believe in them himself. He is not exactly secretive, but could not be altogether trusted. He could easily be led, was very suggestible, moody, and unsettled. He was a great chatterer, conceited and boastful in general, but especially about his physical appearance. He was always wanting to get on and to play an important part in life. His temper was quicker. He was interested in many things, but was superficial and changeable in his tastes. He was excitable and sensitive and quickly boiled over, blushed easily, but did not bear resentment. He had a good deal of luck.

Both brothers are deep sleepers, Erich even more so than Otto. Both perspire remarkably easily. They are moderate drinkers on the whole. Alcohol tires Erich and makes him sleepy; Otto, on the contrary, is bucked up by it. It makes him witty and talkative. Everybody is astonished that such a young man can have "so much intelligence, so much experience, and such ideas". (This is probably homosexual flattery.)

Erich always preferred boys' games, whereas Otto liked to push the perambulator, to play at nurse, or help in the kitchen, and was generally more fond of feminine activities.

His mental development was not opposed to his brother's. Both always got on splendidly together and were always treated exactly alike. They were never jealous of one another. Otto always thought, however, that he got less at meals. When he failed to get his remove at school, Otto was sorry, but only because he was no longer in the same form as his brother. Both brothers agree that this occurrence did not affect his vanity. Nor did it drive him to make greater efforts. Otto was the first to mature sexually from the physical point of view. He masturbated, though not to any great extent, and still does so occasionally. So does Erich. In the latter's case everything was otherwise quite straightforward and normal. He had his first sexual connection at nineteen, and, as his temperament would lead one to expect, has only had three affairs so far. His sexual instinct is normal, though not very powerful. He intends to marry his present girl, and has been walking out with her for nine months without having had any intercourse with her. She is a girl of good family. Outward circumstances are not favourable and Erich does not like awkward situations. He strenuously denies any attraction to his own sex. It disgusts him to think of such a thing. He cannot imagine how anyone could have anything to do with a man. Erich has always been very successful with women and is proud of it.

At puberty Otto admired male forms, although without thinking anything of it and without conscious sexual excitement. At that time he did not indulge in mutual masturbation. He was very fond of bathing. Otto had his first conscious and surprising experience of sexual excitement in the presence of males when he was eighteen years old. He was called to the colours and in a military environment saw for the first time several unclothed young men. He had previously had occasional intercourse with females, but without particularly caring for it. He continued to do so for a time after this first homosexual experience. At the present time he has had nothing to do with women for years. They do not attract him in any way. Otto was always very curious about questions of sex. He read a great deal on the subject, then he consciously sought the company of men and allowed himself to be "seduced". He himself then seduced another young man. He got himself talked about. One day, as he was dawdling along the streets in a suggestive manner, he was taken up by a detective and frankly made a confession without having been obliged to do so. In reality he never was a "fairy". He was given a sentence of fourteen days, which for certain reasons could not be cancelled although those in charge would have liked to do so.

At present Otto is definitely an invert of the passive type. His sexual vanity is considerable; he talks in a painfully skittish manner of his stately figure, shoves out his chest, etc. During his physical examination his behaviour became noticeable owing to its similarity to that of a certain sort of girl. Even when his head was examined, he breathed deeply, made eyes, and indulged in sexual mimicry. It was entirely owing to this that his previous history was brought to light. The examination was being made in the course of a current investigation of twins.

Both twins apparently suffered at birth. Erich had a damaged shoulder from early childhood; Otto's right cheek was flaccid and he suffered from a tic of the face of organic origin. But above all Otto is of lighter build. He has a more slender and rather narrower head and is not nearly so heavy as the athletic Erich, who reminds one of a boxer. The extremities are substantially less developed in Otto than in Erich. Erich also takes one size larger in shoes.

Finally, Otto has definitely less pubic hair, and its upper border is somewhat of the female type, though not extremely so. Above the *mons Veneris* he has the typical female fold, and finally breasts of definitely feminine appearance, as opposed to the masculine conformation of Erich's.

In spite of all differences there is not much doubt that the brothers are monozygotic twins. Apart from their identical complexions they have exactly similar finger-print patterns with the exception of one index-finger. This is very common in monozygotic twins. In spite of all the differences in expression, the resemblances in so many definite characters are so great that they can only be due to monozygotism. They are also of strikingly similar appearance.

This case reveals in twins of the same heredity a definite and comprehensive difference in sexual orienta-tion; one is heterosexual, the other homosexual. This difference corresponds to a similar one between the physical secondary sexual characteristics. Corresponding to these the psychology of one twin is extremely and specifically masculine, whereas that of the other has a strong feminine streak.

Owing to his perverse sexuality and his corresponding lack of self-control, one of the brothers acts contrary to the legal code, whilst his heterosexual twin does not come into conflict with it. Both twins bear the marks of lesions in early childhood, probably received at birth. The heterosexual one has a damaged shoulder, the homo-sexual one is imperfect on one side of the body, which seems to prove a brain lesion, probably of a deep-seated character. An expert cannot help feeling convinced that there is some connection between this brain lesion and his sexual abnormality.

The difference in their behaviour from the legal point of view seems chiefly due to strong physical influences, although in this case, as always, these do not become significant except in connection with particular experiences. The latter would have no effect if they were not brought to bear on a certain type of human material.

2. *Xaver and Johann Ball*

Many years ago Xaver Ball, then twenty-six years old, murdered most brutally a girl who was alleged to be going to have a child by him. His twin brother, who closely resembles him, is now a completely respectable peasant of over fifty. His whole family is decent and hardworking. All the relations have completely unblemished police records.

Ball was sentenced to death, but was reprieved.

I should like at once to state that I would certainly not have considered Ball responsible for his actions. I should at least have had serious doubts as to his fitness to plead; this seems to have been the opinion of one of the three legal experts on the case, and another of them came very near to sharing it.

The whole of the record leaves one with a particularly strong impression that the examining judge did not understand the case. He busily pursued every fact against Ball, but it is obvious that he knew all the time they did not make sense. Even the prosecution was uneasy, and with good reason. In consequence, efforts are now being made to have Ball set free. His sister has not the least fear that if he were set at liberty he would get into

XAVER BALL

trouble. At the time of the crime it was unanimously agreed that Ball must have been mad when he committed it.

This is certainly the first impression one gets from the record. The crime itself was quite unusual. Ball was having an affair with the daughter of a school-teacher. As she already had an illegitimate child by another man she was set on marrying him. He did not wish to marry her and tried to keep free. But he liked girls and now and then got off with one; once attempted sexual intercourse, although with no success. He was stupid and clumsy and could not express himself properly. He was only successful on one occasion after a dance. A few days later the girl told him she was pregnant. He did not believe her. But a couple of months later there was no doubt about it. He went to the woman at whose inn the dance had been given and told her about it. She told others. At that time Ball was not well. He seemed always to be absent-minded, had no appetite, vomited often, and was physically run down. It was thought that there was some connection between the girl's visit and his ill-health; Ball denied it, not altogether unreasonably. He declared that he had been feeling unwell for months previously. He now thought his fellow-workers were making fun of him. This was not at all true. On the contrary, they tried to console him, because they thought he was so depressed by the dread of having to pay on a paternity order. But all their words seemed to him so many pin-pricks. On the afternoon of the crime he went to sleep on a chair at an inn. Then he went away, waited for the girl, and when she came asked her to accompany him. She did so. They went out on to the highway. Ball

L

started to argue with her about her pregnancy. She answered angrily. Then he boxed her ears. She hit back, whereupon he threw her to the ground and started to throttle her. A man with a dagger-stick arrived on the scene; Ball let the girl go and the man took her under his protection. Ball followed them and kept on inviting her to go home with him. Then suddenly he pulled out his knife and attacked her blindly, in spite of the presence of the other man. He ran away and stumbled, wounding himself in his fall with the knife he was still carrying open in his hand. In passing the place where he had tried to throttle the girl, he picked up the kerchief she had dropped and hid it under a bush. Then he went home and shortly afterwards a policeman found him asleep in bed with his hands still bloody. The policeman declared Ball was shamming, but his landlady, who knew him well, was convinced that his behaviour was genuine. She thought he must have slept. His behaviour after the deed was dull and bemused. He could not take in the situation —the girl died shortly after—and observers in the institution diagnosed pseudo-dementia. He could not follow the judgment. He had to be told afterwards that he had been condemned to death. The photograph of him taken in prison shows an unusually empty, groping, and at the same time depressive expression.

His prehistory was as follows: Ball was the first-born and at birth had a swelling on his head as large as a hen's egg, which later disappeared. When he was between two and four he was tossed by a cow, and in consequence suffered for several years from nightly fits, described as epileptiform in character. They had disappeared by the time he started to go to school. At ten he showed curious symptoms of compulsion neurosis, which expressed itself in a passion for tidiness. These also disappeared in due course. A few years before the murder he once fell from the floor of a barn onto the threshing-floor, a distance of 6 metres. He was unconscious and was ill for a week. The records do not reveal any definitely abnormal conditions, nor could his sister, a very intelligent woman, give me any definite information. Neither could Ball himself, who certainly impresses one as of limited and clumsy intelligence. But his letters and the information given by his acquaintances prove that his conduct has always been remarkably uneven.

In appearance he is strikingly like his brother. No one could tell the two apart; only Xaver's "look" was different; he had a "crooked glance", just like one of his uncles—"a curious man". Their former teacher wrote: "What is true of one is true of the other . . . nothing bad to be said about their behaviour. On the other hand, their abilities were very slight, and both of them had so little sense that I once said to a colleague, 'Those brothers seem to have divided up their intelligence also'." They were always among the stupidest boys at school. It is said that another teacher gave them highest marks for conduct —although on the street they behaved like regular urchins. This teacher thought Xaver was less "open". This agrees with his "crooked look". His twin could talk, was more lively, and suited to the profession of innkeeping, although he was also lazier. Xaver could not talk to people, was monosyllabic, often rough, and blazed up easily. But he was very industrious and orderly, though no doubt the more stupid of the two.

Once both twins together were accused of rape. They

arrived, probably drunk, at a very doubtful female's and proposed sexual intercourse to her. The prosecution was dropped because they had obviously committed no crime.

Ball now has a right ptosis and a paresis of the internus muscle of the right eye. The tongue easily drops to the right. According to himself he sometimes sees double. One wonders how long this has been the case. The photograph referred to, when he was young, suggests a paresis of the right internus. His "crooked" look must be remembered. His behaviour in prison was in general excellent.

Personal impressions and his letters reveal Xaver Ball as far from enjoying good health. My opinion is that he was suffering from traumatic effects which revealed themselves for a time in epileptiform fits and later in a tendency to abnormal states, in one of which he committed the murder. All information agrees in indicating a semiconscious condition; his sleep before and after the deed is remarkable, and so is the deed itself with its several quite incomprehensible details.

I do not doubt that our assumptions made after the event, which, by the way, agree with the one intelligent expert opinion, are right. The case reveals disagreement between the behaviour of the twins; but it is due to gross exterior influences and not to a difference in personality due to social or mental causes. At the same time this discordant observation is certainly not an argument against the great importance of innate tendencies for the perpetration of crime.

3. Otto and Ludwig Landsknecht

No one would take these two brothers, now forty-one, for twins, and it would be quite impossible to mistake them for one another. Ludwig's neck and face are framed in a weird soft goitre, which joins the face, that looks too small for its setting, straightway to the body. He is also much fatter than his brother, who shows no signs of goitre. A closer inspection, however, reveals very definite resemblances in the features, and the growth and form of the hair. The eye-colour is similar and their hair, now turning grey, only differs in tint by a shade. The facial hair is similar. Otto is not only thinner but also more finely built. His body is not so broad and his chest is not so deep as his brother's.

The latter has always been the case, and it was therefore always possible to tell the brothers apart if one saw them together. Their parents and teachers were hardly ever mistaken. Strangers sometimes were, provided they saw one of the twins by himself. The resemblance on their photographs taken in childhood is greater than it is now, but even on these there are definite differences, not only in their shape and size, but also in expression.

Their tendencies to illnesses were also different, apart from the development of goitre, which Ludwig derives from his mother. He went through a series of severe attacks of rheumatism of the joints. The first one occurred during his military service. He was down with it for several weeks, but was not discharged on account of it. He had a particularly serious attack during the war. On that occasion the doctors gave him up. He was delirious, as was also the case during a heavy attack of influenza he suffered in 1919 or 1920. At about the same time he had gone back home and then began to get fatter still, gradually developing his goitre. It is possible that at that time he might also have had encephalitis.

But this cannot be stated with certainty, as there is no proof of actual nervous disorders in consequence.

Otto always escaped all the more serious ailments. He was a heavy drinker and still is, whereas Ludwig nowadays has practically given up beer. He previously drank between five and six measures a day at most, and although less than this occasionally, still took quite a fair amount. Otto, however, always beat him at it and still takes his four measures daily.

The brothers were born in poor circumstances. Their father was a manservant. He was a heavy drinker and was twice sentenced for wounding. He was a sullen, close man; according to Otto he had no affection for his family, whereas Ludwig asserts that he had his good days and was a decent fellow. Both sons praise their mother and describe her as a capable, kind, warm-hearted, and very industrious woman who brought her children up well. The father died before he was sixty, no one quite knew from what cause. Their mother lived to seventy-one. She was never exactly ill, but during her last three years she got thinner and thinner, in spite of the best food, and without suffering from any actual illness she gradually broke down. She gave birth to sixteen or nineteen children, of whom, however, only four are alive, one son having been killed in an accident at twenty. All the other children died in infancy. The children are not very closely in touch with one another. They know almost nothing of those of their father's first marriage. The twins never got on particularly well together, a very rare phenomenon in monozygotics. They never exactly quarrelled nor interfered with one another, but they always had different aims, another unusual trait in monozygotic twins. No special reason was given to account for it; it just had been so for as long as they could remember.

Ludwig was born first, Otto a few minutes later. From the very first Ludwig was fatter and probably also quieter, and so he remained. Neither was ever or hardly ever ill in infancy, or as school-children, and both developed normally. At school Otto was always better than Ludwig, although not particularly good. In his last form he was placed eighteenth of twenty-six boys. Ludwig, on the other hand, failed to get his remove. He attributed this to his laziness, but that did not alter the fact that Otto was always the better scholar. Ludwig was not apparently jealous of him on that account.

Otto was always the gayer of the two and had "a clever tongue in his head". He used it a great deal too, liked company, and was fond of swanking. Ludwig, on the other hand, was more serious and settled, more dependable, but not nearly such a good talker. He did not care for company, lived mostly by himself, and preferred to stay at home, without, however, being of a misanthropic turn of mind. Their lives reveal the differences in their temperaments quite clearly. Both had to earn money as soon as they left school. They could not afford to learn a trade. But Ludwig soon found a permanent job. Before his military service, after he had served it, until the war, and again after this, he was a workman and soon became a foreman employed by a very big concern, which temporarily came to a standstill owing to the French occupation. Ludwig could have stayed on, but he preferred to go back to his home because he thought the future seemed too uncertain where he was. After a short period of unemployment, during which he was also ill, he got a post with a municipal council, where he feels happy and has remunerative and agreeable work.

Otto, on the other hand, was at first a farm-labourer and later enlisted in the Army. But he was dismissed from it because he fell so deeply in love with a girl that he was absent without leave for several days on end. He was given twenty-one days' close confinement to barracks and then left his regiment. Ludwig had had no such ambitions. He just did his two years' compulsory service, during which, unlike his brother, he won his badge for shooting, and then returned to his job. He married very soon and is on excellent terms with his wife, by whom he has one child. In recent years he has adopted a child whom he loves tenderly. His sexual life was never very active.

Otto, on the contrary, has not only an illegitimate child, begotten during his military service, but since his marriage he has also become the father of another woman's child. He married later than Otto. He does not get on badly with his wife, by whom he has two children, born at a considerable interval from one another.

Both brothers served in the war. At an early stage Ludwig was very badly wounded in the hand and spent nearly a year in hospital, after which his factory asked to have him back. Otto earned the Iron Cross of the second class, was taken prisoner in 1917, and did not return home until 1920.

After the war both joined the Communist Party, Ludwig only for a very short time. He was forced to do so by the conditions prevailing in his workshop at the time. He very soon retired altogether from political life and now is no longer a party member nor wants to have anything more to do with it.

Otto's destiny, on the other hand, was sealed by his "oratorial gifts", his temperament, and his greater intelligence, coupled with his love of drinking. He soon became the local leader of the Factory Workers' Union, and in this post had to do a lot of speaking, sitting about in public-houses and saloons, and collecting of money. He managed the speaking very well, and the drinking too; he drank far too much and also went about with women. Finally, the accounts were out—for a very large sum. One day, when he was already beginning to be suspected, he alleged that a theft had been committed in his office, but he managed so that all clues to the theft were destroyed. The inquiry which was now started showed up his large defalcations and also the fact that he had forged signatures in at least two cases and that he had entered up expenses for bogus journeys. Otto had plenty of excuses, but had to admit the signatures. Nevertheless he tried to put down most of the accusations to political enmity. The court came to a different con- clusion, certainly the right one, but assumed that part of the missing funds had simply dribbled away and also took into consideration the fact that Otto lacked the preliminary training for his post and had had very great temptations. He only received six months for breach of trust, embezzlement, and falsifying documents. He behaved quite well during his imprisonment and did not make a bad impression. Nevertheless, during the mental examination, he told a pack of lies, boasted of distinctions he had not got, as well as of a higher grade in the service than he actually held, and high marks at school.

His sentence pulled him right down. He now lives in the poorest circumstances in a miserable quarter of the town. His wife has to help to earn money. He himself has a very hard job, at which he works unremittingly. The members of his one-time party are now his enemies, not only because of his crime, but especially because he too has left the party.

Ludwig, on the other hand, lives in a very good apartment house. His home is as clean as a new pin, he is contented with his work, happy with his wife and children, without great ambition, and a picture of complete reliability and friendliness.

One might doubt the monozygotism of the Landsknecht brothers in view of the considerable somatic differences, those in their characters and temperaments, together with their unusually indifferent relationship to one another. Nevertheless the resemblances between them seem to me to predominate. In the case of ordinary brothers they would be exceedingly unusual. I have therefore classed this pair with the discordant monozygotics, although they might be put in the group of those not to be positively classified. Nevertheless I think I am justified in doing so.

There is practically nothing more to add to this account of them. Otto's offence was a typical crime of opportunity, but it consisted of a chain of actions which his twin-brother, whose temperament would never have got him into Otto's situation, could hardly have committed. Without his particular mental make-up, Otto would not have reached such a prominent post; without his love of drink and strong sexual impulses he would hardly have taken the moneys entrusted to him. The very characteristics which enabled Otto to attain the situation which led to his downfall are just those which differentiate him from the brother he otherwise so closely resembles. It is not possible to determine how the mental differences between them arose and developed. But one must emphasise that these mental differences correspond to very considerable physical ones, partly such differences (goitre) as have some connection with mental ones. Human souls never fly about without bodies.

V

CONCLUSION

In the first part of these investigations we applied the Twin method with regard to criminals in a purely statistical manner. With the help of the records we ascertained in the case of all available twins whether they themselves and their fellow-twins had come into conflict with the law or not. In every single case we also endeavoured to find out conclusively whether we were dealing with monozygotic twins, i.e. those with the same heredity, or dizygotic pairs, i.e. those with different heredity. In addition we confined ourselves exclusively to those of the same sex and such pairs of whom at least one partner had been sentenced.

Largely with the help of the Bavarian Ministry of Justice and the Institute of Criminal Biology at Straubing Prison we found thirty pairs of twins, of whom thirteen were monozygotics and seventeen were dizygotics. Of the thirteen monozygotic pairs, both twins had been sentenced in ten cases, and in three cases only one twin had come in conflict with the law while the other had not done so. Of the seventeen dizygotic pairs, both twins had only been sentenced in two cases, whilst in all the rest only one twin had come before the courts whilst the other had not. In addition, a comparison between the criminality of dizygotic twins with that reckoned out of a large material of the criminality of ordinary brothers and sisters showed that both of a pair of dizygotic twins were not sentenced more frequently than was to be expected.

Even allowing for all necessary restrictions, which will be gone into later, these facts show quite definitely that under our present social conditions heredity does play a rôle of paramount importance in making the criminal; certainly a far greater rôle than many are prepared to admit.

Our rough figures also permit the conclusion that heredity alone is not exclusively a cause of criminality, but that one must also allow a certain amount for environmental influences. Even our monozygotic pairs did not by any means show complete agreement in their attitudes to crime. The fact that in about one-quarter of the cases only one of the monozygotic twins was sentenced must be interpreted as showing that in these cases some environmental influence or other determined the criminal behaviour.

This statistical result, clear as it is, is still somewhat unsatisfactory. We should have nothing more to say if we had counted out any sort of illnesses or pathological states. Crime, however, cannot be interpreted merely as the result of given biological factors; it is not a purely biological phenomenon which ceases with the criminal. It also presents a social picture, and as such must always have a social background. We could easily imagine a state of society in which a whole series of actions which we now punish as misdeeds and crimes would not fall under the category of social offences. There are other standards, in addition to biological ones, by which a man gets classed as a lawbreaker. One might even object that we had applied a scientific method to material quite unsuitable for it.

Now, although no serious person really doubts that we must first look for the causes of crime in the criminal, i.e. in biological material, the circumstances nevertheless demand that the roughest statistical results should be amplified by detailed individual information which permits a closer investigation, particularly into the environmental influences.

Here the dizygotic pairs, particularly the discordant ones, cannot help us very much. We saw that the criminal members of such pairs had committed the most various misdeeds. Several of them were habitual criminals, whereas their twins had fitted into the social scheme without trouble, and had even got on. It is worth mentioning that in a number of cases it was not the other twin but other sibs who had been in trouble. This fact can be interpreted either to postulate an unusually bad environment or else in favour of the view that in the stocks in question particularly strong hereditary tendencies to anti-social behaviour were being handed on. Both points of view emphasise the relevance of the other twin's non-criminal conduct and the importance of the innate tendencies with which each separate individual enters society.

We might have expected more conclusive information from the concordant dizygotic pairs. Unfortunately our investigations in these cases met with considerable obstacles; in both of them we were dealing with exceptional circumstances. The records obviously showed that both pairs of twins differed in the manner and extent of their crimes. We also know that there were considerable differences of personality between the twins in both cases. But apart from these facts we learnt little that was certain. It is, however, worth emphasising that in the case of one pair we could not help suspecting a common hereditary venereal infection. If this was the fact it might be that we were not dealing in this case so much with innate tendencies to crime as with the results of considerable brain lesions, which, as we know, often predispose to anti-social behaviour. In the case of the second pair it is worth noting that another brother had a heavy criminal record. With due reservation this might lead us to assume a strong inheritance of anti-social tendencies. It is even more noteworthy that the criminal activities of one of the twins resemble those of his third brother much more closely than those of the other twin, who only for a short time committed a series of small misdemeanours, possibly owing to a biological derangement of a temporary character.

The estimation of the extent of the influence of environmental causes of crime should be greatly assisted by a study of the discordant monozygotic couples. If we assume the same innate characteristics, as we may do in these cases, they should only have a subordinate influence in determining the criminality of one of the pair. The chief part should be due to external influences, and the life-histories of the twins should clearly reveal this fact. But our observations contradicted most definitely our expectations of finding social and mental factors chiefly responsible for their criminality. In at least two out of three cases the criminal twins, and they alone, had suffered serious brain lesions; it is possible to conclude that the crimes in question were actually among the consequences of these lesions. In the case of one, a murderer, we were almost certainly dealing with a traumatic epileptic, who committed his dreadful deed when in a pathological condition. The other, a miserable invert, was not only mentally different from his twin, but revealed the physical signs of his abnormal sexuality. The typical mental traits which accompany these physical ones were those which put him in a separate class from his brother and also cause the irresponsibility which leads him into trouble. The cause of these differences between the twins was obviously a serious birth injury, the marks of which both still bear to this very day.

The third discordant monozygotic pair present a very different picture. In this case it is impossible to discount the facts of the social position of the criminal twin, owing to which he had charge of large sums of money, the feeling of power it gave him, his lack of loyalty and of previous education. These observations reveal very clearly how complicated are the various causes of criminal behaviour. We must assume that a definite difference in personality between the twins was responsible for the fact that this particular one attained the position he did. The origin of this difference is unknown to us, but it can certainly be traced back to earliest boyhood. His greater intelligence, his more vivacious temperament, his superior "gift of the gab" were the causes of his getting the job. It is noteworthy that in this case too we find physical bases for the differences in character. The greater degree of sexuality, which differentiates the criminal from his twin brother, is in itself a predisposition to infidelity, and finally his heavy alcoholism, due partly to tempera-ment and partly to his social position, enabled Lands-knecht to break down various inhibitions sufficiently to make his misdeeds possible. So that when we look into the matter closely we find in this case also that the social factors and those of experience are relegated to a minor place, although they cannot be discounted.

The concordant monozygotic pairs should reveal to us the similar effect of similar innate tendencies, whilst the differences in their cases should enable us to estimate the importance of environmental factors. Nevertheless, if we consider their histories from this point of view, we are struck by finding complete agreement, far beyond what we might have reasonably expected, in the behaviour of a whole number of pairs. I only wish to remind the reader of the brothers Heufelder, Meister, Lauterbach, and Ostertag, as well as the Dieners and Maats, and the sisters Messer. In all these cases the type of crime is absolutely similar, the criminal careers begin at about the same age, and the behaviour of both in court and in prison corresponds absolutely. The Heufelders are old burglars, both of whom have been behind iron bars for nearly two decades and both of whom show paranoiac symptoms in prison. Both brothers Meister commit puerile offences against the laws of property, and both in prison suffer deeply owing to their terrified imaginations. The Lauterbachs are quite unusual swindlers, crooks almost of genius, who keep the upper hand even in court, and whose "respectability" in prison is almost as great as their unblushing impudence. Both brothers Ostertag have just too little sense and will-power, at least in view of the ambitions induced in them by their happy, prosperous youth. The two Dieners, guttersnipes, but good fellows at heart, cannot stand alcohol; it makes them rabid and draws the knives from their pockets. The Maat brothers have not a scrap of affection for any-one in the whole wide world except their own unpleasant selves. Their abnormal sexuality leads them into inti-mate relationships, but even these only seem to be of

M

value to them if they can exploit those with whom they are involved. Finally, the sisters Messer suffer from a degree of nymphomania which must be rare. In all these cases we see the results of the common law which binds these pairs of twins to one another.

At the same time we must consider a possible objection, or at least ask ourselves a question which is of the greatest importance for the interpretation of our results. Is the close resemblance in the criminal behaviour of these twins not perhaps due to common experiences or mutual influence? In the case of the Ostertag twins we were certainly of the opinion that they would hardly have committed their swindles had it not occurred to them to set up in partnership. It seemed as if separately each one would have had sufficient powers of resistance to adapt himself to his social environment, but that the greater irresponsibility of the one, combined with the other's greater laziness, led to the downfall of their common activities. But the fact that these particular twins came to work together was probably due to accidental causes. When in difficulties one of the brothers soon found a colleague of the same type prepared to assist him in other illegal actions, and the other brother was probably lucky in having a stronger-willed wife who stuck to him throughout his troubles. Further facts incline one to the view that the influence of the biological rhythm predominates: after their first mischievousness during puberty they seemed to settle down for a time; now, after more than fifteen years, both have put on flesh and have also developed diabetes. Not very much remains which can be attributed to definite mutual influences. In the other cases there is even less question of such possibilities. The Heufelders never got on well together and both went the same way independently; exactly the same is true of the Meisters, who were far apart when their misfortunes fell upon them, just as they were when they suddenly developed appendicitis and when they ran away from their jobs. The most that can be said from this point of view about the Lauterbachs is that one brother copied from the other his particular method of swindling. But long before this he had proved that he could invent schemes of his own, and his luck and his completely shady nature were revealed more than once. I need hardly mention the Dieners here, and as for the Maats, one may take their word for it that each discovered his perverse instincts independently of the other. The innate sexual activity of each of the Messer sisters only showed itself fully long after they had been separated and sent to different institutions. One of them ran riot after and in spite of marriage, the other indulged in endless non-matrimonial affairs. If these life-histories are studied without prejudice, it can hardly be said that they reveal a preponderant mutual influence of the respective pairs.

At the same time this does not eliminate the possibility that both twins were subjected to similar mental influences in early childhood, which, according to their similar natures, determined their similar destinies. But it is perhaps unnecessary to go closely into this matter, as according to the well-known theory the influences in question appear to recede farther and farther back to the earliest and dimmest beginnings of childhood. Even if we do take this suggestion into account, we must presuppose similar innate tendencies, which are still decisive. According to general experience, however, twins are not invariably treated in exactly the same way and do reveal various mental differences. In spite of this they ultimately behave pretty similarly when faced with important situations in later life. I have observed this over and over again in my other studies of twins and took it to be the expression of the fact that the superficial differences were superimposed on a similar innate material which determined their general conduct on all decisive occasions in their lives. Even our criminal twins do sometimes show fairly definite differences in their mental make-up, but when it comes to their criminal behaviour, these differences either disappear or have only a minor influence. All this, no doubt, will hardly convince opponents whose minds are made up before their observations have given them the facts.

Let us therefore stick to the pair which were separated earliest. I refer to the Schweizer twins, who lost their excellent mother when they were eight years old, and were then subjected to very different educational influences. The more obvious facts in the stories of their later lives might at first lead us to suppose that the differences in their experiences during childhood had been of the greatest importance for the development of their personalities. Even so there are plenty of similarities in their conduct. After seven years' separation both were punished when living in two different towns for having stayed away from school. Then, whilst one of them took to vagrancy and to unrestrained and stupid offences against property, the other was not a particularly good apprentice to his kind old foster-father and master. At an early date he started to have love-affairs, to smoke far too much, and then threatened to murder his unfaithful girl friend's new lover, finally wounding him. Subsequently he ran away in the most ungrateful manner, just when he was most urgently required by his master. The first marriages of both revealed crazy conditions. There is not much to choose between the behaviour of one who, on his wedding-night, went to bed with a woman other than his wife, and that of the other in whose presence his wife misconducted herself with a friend and who, after his separation, though before his divorce, had illegitimate children by two different women. Finally, this broken-down fellow, who had not a whole garment to his name, and who had to be fetched home by the foster-father he so ungratefully deserted, who drank twenty-four glasses of beer in a day, can hardly be considered a cut above his brother, who was always being picked up drunk in the gutter. Though life may have led them far apart, they are nevertheless united by the identical lack of will-power which determines the fate of both. This is what controls their lives rather than experiences in early childhood. One of them finally married a woman whose will-power alone keeps him out of prison, the other was less lucky and has fallen to the moral level of his last lady-love. In spite of all this there are, of course, outward differences which are fairly impressive. Only they have no connection with that particular growth of personality due to experience; they are not capable of development; they are merely the outward garments in which their personalities are wrapped up.

Even so, these small differences cannot be summarily dismissed. Such details of social behaviour do happen to decide whether a person ends up in gaol or not. Our observations reveal other similar effects of environmental conditions. One of the brothers Rieder, for example, who is married to a decent woman, leads, if not a distinguished, at least a more or less blameless life. His twin brother on the other hand, had the misfortune to lose his first excellent wife and then to marry a spitfire, so that finally his present kind-hearted partner led him into new temptations, and so to his ruin. The Ostertag brothers also show in the one case the temporary bad influence of an amorous relationship, whereas in the other the facts are reversed.

Nevertheless the circumstances of the Rieder brothers are not so simple as they might appear from the foregoing. Wilhelm not merely acquired his "pincers" and his Frieda, but at the Front he also developed tuberculosis. Whatever the reasons for it may be, this disease does seem to diminish the sufferers' self-control. And in addition he took once more and in a greater degree than ever to alcohol. The particularly evil influence of this revealed itself two decades earlier in the case of his brother Josef, and it is manifest also in the case of the Dieners, the Schweizers, of Wolfgang Lauterbach, and particularly in Georg Krämer, with whom we have still to deal. If we add to this that the Meisters are by no means teetotallers, and that Otto Landsknecht's lack of self-control was also partly due to drink, we have quite an impressive series of part or whole victims of this enemy of mankind, which, of course, is always disguised as a bringer of pleasure and promoter of friendship. In the narrower sense, however, alcohol has neither social nor mental influences, and that is why in many instances the effects of such outward influences, which at first might appear considerable, are shown after a time to fade away.

We have still not given a complete account of all the influences at work on the Rieder twins. Their reaction to their friend's suicide revealed that both were very suggestible. We must therefore take into consideration that Josef was probably not uninfluenced by his year and a quarter in prison, and that this may have been one of the causes of his good conduct in later life. It is a pity that, owing to the fact that the records had been withdrawn before our investigation, we were unable to obtain further details about the Rieder brothers. It is, however, certain that suggestible people are deeply influenced by imprisonment. The Meister brothers remember their prison experiences with horror and are deeply grateful to those who took a sympathetic interest in them during that time. Both were still quite young, as was Josef Reider, when they served their fairly lengthy sentences. The deep impression made on them may be due to this fact. August Heufelder, too, was deeply influenced by his first fairly long period of imprisonment. During the course of it he developed mentally, and even to-day his twin brother of thirty-eight has not got as far in mental progress as August had by the time he was twenty. In spite of this, however, the laws which ruled August Heufelder's inner nature were the stronger.

There is no doubt that both Heufelders suffered bitterly during heir imprisonment. This emerges clearly from their paranoid-paranoiac symptoms and also from their whole conversation. August reached mental maturity through his struggle with his inner problems and terrible mental suffering, just as Adolf's battle "for the right" symbolised for him his inner conflicts. Adolf's rebellion in the penitentiary, as well as the wild revolt of both brothers against discipline towards the end of a lengthy sentence, were other symptoms of these inner conflicts. The pressure of terrible forces working in their souls had to be lightened somehow. Ricarda Huch once said, "Just as a man has to carry the weight of his body about with him, so he has to carry the weight of his soul." In the case of the Heufelder brothers this weight was almost unbearably heavy during their imprisonment. The opposite is true of the Lauterbachs. These twins showed an astonishing adaptability in stepping right out of the greatest luxury straight into the deprivations of prison life. It is true that they obtained all possible favours, but nevertheless the effects of imprisonment glided off them like water off a duck's back. In order to make an impression on them other methods would have had to be found. There was no weight which would not instantly sink in such tenuous material as their minds were made of.

We have not yet dealt with the Krämer brothers, who, although both have been sentenced, are a discordant pair with respect to the nature of their crimes. It has already been mentioned that this discrepancy may be due, in addition to the effects of alcohol, to a serious brain lesion incurred by one of them, which may have shifted his mental and physical development in a different direction from his brother's. Still, both have been in conflict with the law. One might perhaps discount Adolf's theft as a silly boy's prank; I do not think, however, that this would be justifiable. On the contrary, I think it presents a definite problem, possibly the most important problem of our whole investigation.

Ludwig Diener's record revealed, in addition to an act of brutality committed under alcoholic influence, a crime against property. The same is true of Luitpold Schweizer, Josef Rieder, and of Georg Meister. The Heufelder brothers, in addition to their denial of all property rights, occasionally show an unmistakable trend to brutality; August, in an offence against decency and later in a case of wounding; Adolf, when committing his theft with violence, when the terrified woman he had robbed was hung up by the neck by her attackers. The Messer sisters reveal a very definite lack of general self-control as well as abnormal sexuality. The Lauterbachs also were not exactly guardians of morals in sexual affairs; the Maats appear to be not only inverts, but to profit financially by their abnormality. I could give several other instances in this connection. But the Heufelders reveal most distinctly the two types of delinquency.

The same observation can be made in numerous cases investigated which provided a large amount of material concerning the life-histories of habitual criminals. Very often one or the other type of crime predominates, but it is not at all unusual for crimes of brutality and offences against property to coexist to about the same degree, and sexual offences are very often allied to them. This is the case even with people who cannot be summarily dismissed as professional criminals.

Now here I think we have found the biological break-ing-point of which social delinquencies are a result. The inability to resist innate urges never seems to work exclusively in one direction, but seems to be more or less general. In some way or other there seems to be a break-down in curbing or restraining these urges, quite apart from their own strength. This appears to have nothing, or at least nothing directly, to do with the mental superstructure. Individuals of excellent intelligence and even of unusual emotional development are known who, in spite of these and other admirable qualities, again and again go wrong. It is certainly true that those who possess abnormally strong instincts run greater risks in this direction, and so do the feeble-minded and those who show emotional defects, especially those suffering from moral insanity in the closer sense. Yet none of these people need become criminals. In order that this should occur, it seems to be necessary that in some way the instinctive and the directive functions which condition personality should fail to work together safely and usefully, apart from those cases, probably very rare ones, in which crime is regarded as a profession or gradually becomes one.

A similar phenomenon can be observed to occur comparatively late in life, generally as the result of serious brain lesions. Of the greatest interest in this connection are not so much serious pathological conditions as the criminal behaviour resulting from these processes, and which reveals itself at a stage when one cannot clearly detect failure of the intellect or other deteriorations in the sufferer's character. The obvious example is the alteration in social behaviour brought about by *encephalitis epidemica*, or "sleepy sickness", of which we have studied the detrimental effects on so many adolescent victims. Before one is able to trace serious lesions of the nervous system, a failing of intellectual ability, or, at any rate at the onset, defects in emotional relationships, one finds such symptoms. Children who have previously been perfectly good start to lie, to steal, to wander about, to ill-treat their companions, to revolt against all discipline, and even to attack grown-ups, and also to behave in a sexually abnormal manner towards those of their own age. In fact, their whole behaviour becomes anti-social. This phenomenon presents us with a kind of enlarged model of the conduct of a great number of our criminals. It may not be due to chance that young people in particular are altered in this way by encephalitis. Our final social relationships are, on the whole, end results of the development of our personalities, which are being gradually built up during childhood, but which, like other phenomena during their development stages, are particularly unstable and capable of being destroyed. It is also noteworthy that puberty, bringing with it as it does entirely new problems and social tasks, is not merely a particularly critical period for those who are obliged at that time to begin making their way in the world, but is also an extremely critical event for the whole develop-ment of personality. It is at this period that a particularly big step has to be taken from purely instinctive life to self-controlled activities, a step which may easily be missed.

The particular functions which seem to be almost solely damaged in the case of young sufferers from encephalitis are just those which in many criminals have not been completely developed and which seem to be unusually accessible to all possible influences, especially that of alcohol, though possibly also to the toxic effects of tuber-culosis. If, as we may assume from our experiences with encephalitis, the functions in question are general ones, it should not astonish us that lapses of the most diverse kind take place so frequently. Taking other evidence with regard to pathological conditions of the brain into account, it is not difficult to understand why so many prisoners reveal hysterical, paranoiac, and paranoid processes. Finally, this evidence also explains fairly clearly why twins of the same innate tendencies behave similarly in the overwhelming majority of cases. In spite of all superficial differences the deep-seated functions clearly develop in an overwhelmingly similar manner in these twins.

In my opinion Homburger has quite rightly emphasised that in the case of young encephalitis victims we have to deal with a change of behaviour rather than with a change of character. In the case of criminals, matters do not seem very different. The twins we studied reveal characters of the most various kinds. The type of human being assumed by the layman to be "the criminal type" hardly exists among them. The Meisters and the Ostertags, the Dieners and even the Schweizers, the Rieders and the Krämers, are not really "criminals", any more than the Messer sisters. Among them are a whole group of kind-hearted, gentle creatures who would indignantly deny that they had ever intended to become professional criminals. I would go farther and say that not one of them would be capable of planning and carrying out a large crime. They all lack the *will* to crime.

The Heufelders are in a different class, for in their more recent years, at any rate, they quite deliberately adopted burglary as a profession. But even in their case this was not always so, and we know for certain that August—he, at any rate, asserted it, and we believe him —was only forced through penury to gain his living by crime. Adolf is in a different category. He seems to have been altogether changed by the war and to have committed his crimes with a certain amount of professional pride. But even he was probably partly influenced in taking this turning by his experiences in wartime and the bad post-war conditions to which he returned from a long period of demoralising imprisonment. I think it extremely probable that not a few criminals become professionals as August did, simply because our society has no further use for people of his type and with records like his. It is necessary to emphasise the fact that permanent detention would be less of a misery for such people than the constant forcing of them into crime with its accompaniment of shame and harsh privations.

The atmosphere surrounding the Lauterbachs and especially the Maats is a much less agreeable one than that of the Heufelders. The Maats appear to me to belong on the human scrap-heap. Their careers have only just begun. I expect no good from them in the future, even if their intelligence and their cold-bloodedness enable them to discover means of preying on their fellow-creatures which will not bring them within the arm of the law. The Lauterbachs are less evil but more dangerous to society. They are swindlers of the deepest dye, and their aim, probably quite consciously, is simply the shameless exploitation of other human beings. One might perhaps let them go provided one could write their records on their foreheads for everyone to read, and if one could make it impossible for them to propagate their kind.

But even the last-mentioned pairs of twins cannot be classed with such active criminals as those whom Klages defines as devoid of all human feelings or any desire to work; complete egotists for whom nothing counts beyond the satisfaction of their most primitive urges, which include an abnormal and almost instinctive degree of cruelty. Such people are bound to go wrong in any society, because the slightest resistance from outside induces anti-social behaviour on their part. Still, even people of the type of the Lauterbachs and the Maats remain anti-social at bottom, although a favourable destiny may accidentally protect them against conflicts with the criminal law. All the others reveal environmental influences, the Heufelders showing these at their worst. It is true that during the later stages of their careers the environment of the Heufelders was not an average but an abnormal one, due to the cruel counter-measures with which society opposed their own anti-social dealings. In this case one might mention the "guilt" of society, if this expression is permissible with reference to our investigation.

In none of the other cases can we leave environmental influences on the development of criminal behaviour out of account. I will take Karl Diener's manslaughter as a crude example. His alcoholism was not his own doing, but occurred because his constitution subjected him to the effects of our general drinking customs. It was not alone his peculiar habit to have a knife handy in any row. This is a habit he shares with all his countrymen of his own age, not even alone with these, or with people in his own social circle. This custom is an almost innate peculiarity of all old Bavarians, of whatever class they may be, and one they will probably take to the grave with them. The fact, however, that Karl Diener *used* his knife has a very close connection with his social status. A drunken student in similar circumstances would have insulted his opponent to provoke a duel and would have sent him his seconds on the following day. The bodily injuries which are caused in this way, however, do not lead most of those who commit them before the criminal courts.

I could cite similar examples with regard to offences against property. I will only refer briefly to the thefts of intellectual property, which even in the worst cases do not lead to real social outlawry, at least not to the same extent or of such crushing weight as thefts of property of half their importance, quite apart from the fact that the courts hardly ever have to deal with them.

At the same time I have not suggested that one could possibly think—though probably do no more than think —of a social organisation in which offences against property would simply not be worth while even if the proportions of apprehended criminals were a good deal lower than i' is in our own. If we discuss the importance of social influences we simply must do so against the background of the economic system of to-day.

We thus see revealed in addition to innate tendencies environmental influences, some of them of a quite general kind, others to which the individual, unable to escape their pressure, succumbs. Environmental influences are of particular importance for the criminal just because his very nature includes a far greater amount of suggestibility than the average. Thus he very often becomes a helpless victim of any environment in which he happens to find himself.

But the environment itself depends to a very considerable extent on the type of individual concerned.

The personal histories I have given show this very clearly, not so much in the destinies of the separate individuals as through a comparison between the pairs in each case. Not one solitary *twin* managed to get out of the social class in which the other was included. As an example we may take the vain attempt of Luitpold Schweizer to start and to maintain a business of his own —vain in spite of his strong-willed and industrious second wife. Further, I would remind the reader of Otto Landsknecht, who, in spite of all his good qualities and particularly favourable opportunities, tumbled irresistibly from his high position. As an example of the opposite one might take Josef Rieder; but he too remained a member of the working-classes. The two Lauterbachs fell to the depths from their dizzy heights. The Ostertags dropped out of their grandfather's and father's class owing to a pitiful gap between their demands on life and their abilities to satisfy them. Finally, both brothers Maat, although they are at present just managing to cling to the outer circles of the cultured middle-classes, have already fallen far below their original environment, and they will probably do so completely as soon as their very wealthy father withdraws his protection from them. I need hardly mention any of the others.

In contrast to these pairs I would like to draw the reader's attention to the dizygotic twins. Even when both have come in conflict with the law, we have, in one case, at any rate, a difference of at least two classes between a couple of twins. In all the discordant cases they are further separated by the gulf opened by imprisonment between a guilty and an innocent person. But even more noteworthy is the fact that certain individual twins have reached a social position considerably higher than that of their father, whereas their brothers have fallen in the social scale.

It is therefore not merely his original environment which determines the social class to which an individual belongs and the particular temptations to crime which confront him. On the contrary, this itself is determined by his type, which in its turn largely depends on the inner laws which determine his particular tendency to crime. This is a new aspect of the problem for those who insist again and again on penury, misery, and privations as the true causes of social downfall. I may also add that my normal twins very rarely reveal class differences between pairs originally brought up together. I hardly dare hope that this lesson will impress convinced believers in the "environmental theory". There is still the bogy called "society" which makes it possible for anyone to rise or fall.

Types closely related to our subjects are to be found without exception in the large group of psychopathic individuals of all kinds. A large majority of them are weak-willed or will-less. Among the symptoms of such people must be classed their ever-ready tendency to fall into crime, though this does not apply to all cases. Putative criminals constitute only one group of the weak-willed. Numbers of others, who suffer from slight or imaginary disabilities, fill our hospitals or wander about our streets. Masses of them are to be found in professions of recent origin; they are film-actors and supers, pavement artists and hawkers, hole-and-corner reporters and "representatives"; even more particularly wives who find everything too much trouble, and prostitutes who take

N

no real pride in their profession. We find them also in another section of the community whose habits are just as true to type; among those whom we consider particularly praiseworthy, those good, kind creatures who are the defenceless victims of their sympathies and would "give away the shirt off their back". I know a female "criminal" who was driven by sheer kind-heartedness not merely to give away her all and to go hungry in consequence, but who performed abortions gratis and was punished for doing so. Probably these friends of humanity who are thus compelled to act against their own interests are not so rare as we think.

The most closely related individuals to swindlers of the Lauterbach type are found among a large number of hospital patients—namely, hysterical fakers; also in the increasing ranks of income-tax defrauders, among journalists, novelists, and fraudulent freebooters in all professions, but especially, as in the former cases, among women, who harass their families in all sorts of ways. This class also includes a large number of valuable people whose heightened imagination finds a useful outlet in artistic creation. I would only remind the reader of Clemens Brentano, to take an example from another period than our own.

We occasionally see the close inter-relationships of both groups, as exemplified by Ferdinand Meister, who, as time goes on, is more and more frequently in hospital, and the Lauterbachs, who frighten their associates with their mysterious illnesses.

Finally, we must include the large number of suicides, who from sheer weakness set themselves and their fellow-creatures free of them. Up to a point I agree with Von

Hentig, who interprets the fate of these unfortunates as an act which delivers society from its incompetent members. I need not say one can only agree with him up to a point, but I myself do not doubt that the victims of many "sporting" accidents belong to this category. I am particularly reminded of the large number of disgracefully careless motor-cyclists who not only make a nuisance of themselves to everyone by the commotion they most inconsiderately cause at all hours of the day, but who by their methods of driving provide constant danger, of which they are themselves the most frequent victims. As a matter of fact, in these cases the carelessness of society is also to blame. We are all guilty in so far as we tolerate such proceedings, and the same is true of many other "sporting" phenomena.

The non-criminal types who resemble our subjects are very often far less useful socially than the criminals themselves, only they become less obviously burdens on the community. The damage done by most of our subjects would really not be so great without the pernicious influence of alcohol. But this again is the fault of society. So long as we not merely look on but encourage drinking, and systematically lie to ourselves about it, we have no *real* right to inflict heavy punishment on a person who is no different from anyone else. True, the most useful people do not generally succumb to alcohol, but nevertheless among those who do there is many a one worth a good deal more than hundreds of thousands who poison themselves from day to day without apparently seriously evil results to society.

In other directions we must tear down the barriers which to-day still separate the good citizens from the

"criminal". We have discussed above the relationships
between the criminal without will-power and numerous
other social dark horses; but we also noted the connection
between them and certain admirable types who command
our entire respect. Let us merely remember that very
many other psychopathics, although they are not anti-
social in the criminal sense, are so in a much more
troublesome way. Martinets and nagging superiors, who
cause their entire staff constant worry—tyrants of the
home before whom their families tremble; easy-going
creatures who throw all responsibility onto others; all
those numerous men who enter of their own free-will
into erotic relationships with girls below their own class—
all these are not socially really useful people, at least not
in certain important aspects of human affairs. Considering
such cases, we are landed right among average human
beings. But even if we only consider actions forbidden by
law, how many of us can truly claim to be completely
blameless in this respect? I know a young lady who can
afford to spend more on herself in one day than many a
large family has to dispose of. This girl once explained to
me that it gave her particular pleasure to take a tram
without paying her fare, or else to go farther than her
ticket would take her. Probably we all of us occasionally
go beyond our "fare", and for the same reason that so
many criminals commit their first infringement of the
law—namely, because owing to some momentary or
permanent breach in social organisation, an opportunity
is created of which, if we are in the mood to do so, we
take advantage. Some may thus take to crime, others
may not; it simply depends on the average power of our
self-control. Here again, as everywhere in the domain of

psychopathic brain functions, we find an unbroken series ranging from quite normal to pathological cases. The boundary between the two is fraught with social consequences. The fact that their behaviour is not exclusively conditioned by their degree of abnormality constitutes the tragedy of so many criminals who are nevertheless worthy human beings.

Our investigations lead to simple and clear conclusions from the point of view of legal criminological action. If criminal behaviour, as it quite obviously does, depends entirely on the laws governing our own inner selves, there is no point in punishment in the narrower sense. Although it is also the object of punishment to safeguard society, this end is still too much obscured by the means taken to achieve it. This is at any rate the view of the masses, based on their "instinctive" impressions. Nowadays we should regard the safety of society as our only and quite definite object, and act accordingly. We must readjust our general views of justice to this point of view.

We have seen that imprisonment as it is to-day can be a drastic method of education and prevention. We do not know whether it is the best one or not. However much we may alter conditions of imprisonment, we can never abolish it. It is only a question of finding the method which is most effective and least harmful to those who must permanently endure it. A system which converts a man like August Heufelder from an irresponsible into a deliberate criminal should be out of the question. It should be one of society's duties to discover a progressive form of imprisonment which would attempt to give back more and more of his lost independence to the prisoner and to lead him back into everyday life. Other equally worthy tasks seem to me to be the reform of the after-care system for discharged prisoners and an alteration in the general public's attitude to crime.

But three other points strike me as of even more urgent importance. The first is the abolition of the dreadful influence of alcohol. But in this connection we know that in Germany, at any rate, we are still talking to deaf ears.

Secondly, we should make every attempt to discover as early as possible those who must be permanently segregated if society is to be protected from grave damage. The detailed examination of all law-breakers and the thorough training of real experts in this subject are essentials towards this end.

Finally, and this is our most important task, we must take preventive measures. We must try to make it impossible for human beings with positive criminal tendencies to be born. It can be said with a fairly high degree of certainly that there is no means of abolishing by birth-control methods the minor criminals who nowadays throng most of our prisons. For they are the results of cross-breeding, which must take place in order to preserve the diversity of individual types which is an *ad hoc* condition for all human culture. I do think it possible, however, to prevent the development of criminal tendencies, but we shall only be able to do so when we know a great deal more than we do to-day. Our Twin method can merely teach us that the tendencies which lead to anti-social behaviour develop in the domain of heredity. It tells us nothing about the manner in which these tendencies are inherited. We know that such tendencies are occasionally inherited as a whole, but can also be built up by new crosses. If our knowledge in this direction is to go beyond these merely general facts it can only do so by means of the most detailed investigation of families. The closest study of criminal heredity must go hand in hand with the investigation of the criminals themselves.

So we finish at the point from which we started. We see the beginning of what is so urgently needed in the Institute for Criminal Biology founded by the Bavarian Ministry of Justice. Unless such methods are widened and, in particular, deepened, i.e. unless we can obtain the most comprehensive apparatus for dealing with the problem, we shall not reach the goal towards which we are so urgently striving.

For Product Safety Concerns and Information please contact our EU
representative GPSR@taylorandfrancis.com
Taylor & Francis Verlag GmbH, Kaufingerstraße 24, 80331 München, Germany

www.ingramcontent.com/pod-product-compliance
Lightning Source LLC
Chambersburg PA
CBHW050442280326
41932CB00013BA/2213